DIVERSITY OF AESTHETICS: VOLUMES 1–3

Edited by Andreas Petrossiants and Jose Rosales

DIVERSITY OF AESTHETICS: VOLUMES 1–3

*Edited by Andreas Petrossiants
and Jose Rosales*

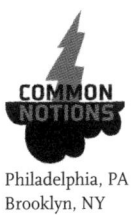

Philadelphia, PA
Brooklyn, NY
commonnotions.org

Diversity of Aesthetics: Volumes 1–3

© Andreas Petrossiants and Jose Rosales, editors
and individual contributors
This edition © 2025 Common Notions

ISBN: 978-1-945335-31-0 | eBook ISBN: 978-1-945335-55-6
Library of Congress Number: 2025933617
10 9 8 7 6 5 4 3 2 1

Common Notions   Common Notions
c/o Interference Archive   c/o Making Worlds Bookstore
314 7th St.   210 S. 45th St.
Brooklyn, NY 11215   Philadelphia, PA 19104

www.commonnotions.org
info@commonnotions.org

Discounted bulk quantities of our books are available for organizing, educational, or fundraising purposes. Please contact Common Notions at the address above for more information.

Cover design by Josh MacPhee
Layout design and typesetting by Suba Murugan
Printed by union labor in Canada on acid-free paper

For Marina Vishmidt (1976–2024)

CONTENTS

INTRODUCTION

Andreas Petrossiants and Jose Rosales

At the end of 2019, we began organizing a series of discussions to be held at the Emily Harvey Foundation (EHF) in New York City planned for March 2020.[1] As structuring principles, we envisioned several meetings and assemblies that would take up Marina Vishmidt's notion of "infrastructural critique" and the notion of destituent insurrection, intending to bring together militant theoretical currents and lessons learned from social movements in and against the art sector.[2] Though the events themselves were canceled due to the pandemic, our conversations continued and developed, including insights gained from encounters with formations like Strike MoMA and the Art Workers' Inquiry (with whom we later held a workers' inquiry about looting in 2023), as well as broader events, primarily the George Floyd rebellion. Rather than live discussions, we decided to organize, print, and distribute three small books prioritizing collaboration across all facets of their production.

From the get-go, we agreed that the volumes would all take the form of roundtable conversations, that they would be recorded live and then edited collaboratively with the participants, and that we would stop at three, limiting the project's scope rather than aspiring for longevity. This was not to be an exercise in building an institution but rather one of sharing in the various conspiratorial anti-institutional and insurgent "speculative" practices we have taken part in.[3] Common to all three volumes is a commitment to re-thinking the relationship between forms of critique and forms of struggle undertaken by collective social practices. We intended to help cultivate spaces of conversation and reflection to carry us through the liberal and fascist counterinsurgencies gaining strength from 2020 through the present. From Shellyne Rodriguez's comments on mass layoffs at cultural institutions during the pandemic in Volume 1, to Jose Rosales and Iman Ganji's discussions about labor insurgency in the Iranian oil sector in Volume 2, to Saidiya Hartman's remarks on the displacement of working and poor communities of color in Harlem in Volume 3, among the many through lines that emerged across the volumes, one can find an incomplete periodization of the "post"-COVID-19 years and the intensification of existing crises of surplus.[4]

Over the last three years we have been lucky enough to stock the books at stores and infoshops across North America, and in Europe thanks to Dabartis (PDFs have moved yet further), to contribute copies to autonomous reading groups and university seminars, and host events in New York (at Woodbine and the EHF), Berlin (b_books), and Vienna (Academy of Fine Arts). After tabling with Common Notions at the New York City Anarchist Book Fair in 2022 and 2023, we asked if they would be interested in collaborating with us on a combined edition, and we are grateful to them for agreeing to embark on this final iteration of the project with us.

Marina Vishmidt, who spoke with Jose at the Vienna launch of Volume 3 in March 2024, had agreed to write an afterword to this present collection. It is with great sadness and grief that we finalized this book after Marina passed away in April 2024. In lieu of an afterword or conclusion, at the end of this book, we have decided to reprint her (as always) incisive comments and crucial questions that she posed that evening in Vienna, and the beginnings of our attempt to think through those questions with her. As many friends have written in the wake of Marina's passing, our conversations and engagement with her prolific oeuvre are only getting started. And as Kerstin Stakemeier puts it, Marina has left us "cues" with which to think, conspire, and organize.[5] Because Marina's notions of infrastructural critique and radical, anticapitalist speculation are so central to the conception of the volumes, this project is co-authored with her. May this book be just one seed in the wider forest of insurgent thought and action that Marina inspired!

In this introduction we briefly summarize some key points from the three volumes and reproduce an abbreviated version of a talk that Jose presented during the event with Marina in Vienna. That talk expands on discussions from Volume 3, the topic of which is "looting," to analyze the mediation and continuation of the ongoing genocide in Gaza. While we have lightly edited the text from each of the volumes to correct for previous inaccuracies, we have not significantly edited the content of any of the conversations, so they all remain documents of their respective moments.

THE VOLUMES

Volume 1, *Inside and Outside: Infrastructures of Critique* (2021), a conversation between Michael Rakowitz, Shellyne Rodriguez, Stevphen Shukaitis, and Andreas, addresses the relations between social movements, artistic production, and the thorny question of art's valorization. It was released following ten weeks of direct action against the Museum of Modern Art (MoMA) organized under the banner of Strike MoMA, and functions as a pretext for complicating and further developing the ideas, experiences, and practices witnessed over the course of those weeks as well as from other social movements within and against the art sector.

The immediate reason that different contingents undertook multiple avenues of resistance against the MoMA in 2020 and 2021 was the fact that the main profiteer in the US from private prisons sits on the MoMA board. But beyond this single concern, Strike MoMA took wider aim at the museum as an institution which, aside from being an apparatus of counterinsurgency, functions as a key lever in the global, racialized, gendered capitalist mode of governance. Unlike other recent movements that have taken place in museums across NYC, this was not solely about targeting one or several board members nor about calling for specific reforms, but was about questioning the role of the institution in wider infrastructures of incarceration and the Capitolocene, actualizing infrastructures for "post-MoMA futures." It was also a pedagogical movement, invested in producing alternate forms of collective learning through assemblies, working groups, seminars, walking tours, and teach-ins.

In the first volume, the participants discussed their experiences working and organizing as different types of cultural workers and how to use the supposed autonomy of art as a precept for radical action rather than an excuse for surrender. In other words, the conversation is an open session of fugitive planning (as are all the volumes), pointing towards what Andreas has since proposed calling "destituent art," which does "not signal a turn to a productive pessimism—that all creative work is already subsumed, for example—but that the cultivation of destituent power actualizes and is actualized by the aesthetic production of places of action after the refusal of power as it exists."[6]

In our earliest discussions, the second volume was intended to explicitly broach the topic of destitution, but we were inspired by the work that Jose and Iman Ganji were undertaking on labor militancy in Iran to focus on a specific case of insurrectionary activity in the Global South.[7] The second volume, with Claire Fontaine, Iman Ganji, and Jose, is a conversation on Claire Fontaine's series of multilingual neon works titled *Foreigners Everywhere*, which gives the volume its title, as well as their notion of the "human strike." The phrase "foreigners everywhere" is borrowed from an anti-racist, anarchist collective from Turin, while "human strike" is Claire Fontaine's term for conceiving of various modes of collective dis-identification with the social position by which subjects have been interpellated. (In a way, this relates to destituent power's "desubjectivization" from the roles assigned by the racialized and gendered capitalist mode of production.)

The original cover of Volume 2 reproduces "foreigners everywhere" in Farsi and Tagalog, languages in which the series of works had not appeared before. This volume presents what is to our knowledge the first discussion about Claire Fontaine's theory by participants of a social movement in the Global South (Iran). As an afterword to the second volume, we reprinted an article by Iman and Jose on the 2021 general strike by zero-hour contract workers in Iran's oil industry and the effects it had on the rest of Iranian society. It was due to this mass mobilization, which emerged out of solidarity with precarious workers within the industry, that Iman and Jose wager that this kind of coordinated mobilization across so many different social groups carried within itself the political preconditions for the realization of a "human strike."

Lastly, Volume 3, *Looting*, with Saidiya Hartman, Christina Sharpe, Rinaldo Walcott, and Vicky Osterweil, came out two years after the George Floyd rebellion and seeks to understand recent ruptures and continuities with mass antiracist protests in the US. From the 2014 Ferguson uprising onwards, it has not been uncommon to encounter a (leftist) position that self-identifies as antiracist and claims to "support the movement" but for whom looting is a step too far. This type of moral critique of looting reappears with every upward swing in mass insurrectionary fervor. As Vicky aptly summarizes, criticism of this kind not only obscures the actually existing opportunities for the creation of solidarity with others but also effectively hinders any prospect of building up a larger street movement.[8] Furthermore, such moral criticism cannot account for what Hartman, Sharpe, and Walcott refer to as "black sociality," or instances wherein certain modalities of black life reproduce themselves on the basis of a total disregard for capitalist abstractions. Interestingly, the level of popular support for insurrectionary activity during the George Floyd rebellion significantly increased relative to both Ferguson (2014) and Baltimore (2015). On June 3, 2020, *Newsweek* reported that 54 percent of Americans considered that burning down the 3rd Precinct of the Minneapolis Police Department was "justified in response to George Floyd's death."[9] For context, this is more support than any US presidential candidate has received in the last forty years.[10] Thus, during the opening phase of the 2020 uprising, support for the rebellion and the desire for abolishing the police took on a *mass* character. The months that followed saw successive waves of local, regional, and state counterinsurgency, resulting in a shift in popular discourse away from abolition and toward "defunding" the police. Acknowledging the distance between the summer of 2020 and the third volume in 2023, *Looting* takes stock of the revolutionary measures the public are willing to support *and* the statist recuperation that reorients rebellion toward policy reforms, such as diversity, equity, and inclusion. While planning the volume, we asked: is looting the only form of property theft that no longer presupposes the property-form? Marina generatively thinks with and against this formulation in the concluding section of this book.

FROM MINNEAPOLIS TO GAZA

If we compare the summer of 2020 to the time of writing this introduction during summer 2024, the figure of the non-accumulative looter seems to have all but disappeared from public view. And yet, on March 6, 2024, UN World Food Programme (WFP) aid workers reported that "after being held at an Israeli army checkpoint for several hours," a fourteen-truck aid convoy destined for northern Gaza was forced to turn back. According to the aid workers, after being denied entry into northern Gaza, the convoy "was attacked and 200 tonnes of food [were] *looted* by 'a large crowd of desperate people.'"[11]

This use of the word "looting" demonstrates how the term can be employed to nominatively enforce the boundaries of private property. In this instance, the invocation of the word "looting" reinforces which forms of dispossession are acceptable to the global terms of order. Given the absence of any obvious correlation between word ("looter") and the action that is being described (Palestinians in Gaza defending against genocide), several other signifiers come to mind. For example, we could describe this scene as one of people whose refusal of death means seizing whatever means of subsistence is available to them—images, thus, not of desperation, but of a people defending against the oblivion that is the logical conclusion to every project of genocide, past and present. If Gazans who haven't eaten in weeks are called "looters" when they are merely seeking the means to satisfy their hunger, what vocabulary remains for describing the countless images of IDF/IOF forces rummaging through Palestinian homes while mockingly displaying articles of clothing taken from the closets of displaced or murdered people?

Thus, implied in *The Guardian*'s use of the word "looting" is the description of Palestinians in Gaza as unruly and, therefore, proof of their being "unfit for democratic self-governance." This is similar to how in Volume 3, Hartman discusses the logics that legitimized the looting of the African continent by regimes of Euro-US white supremacy and how Sharpe discusses racialized coverage of people surviving following Hurricane Katrina. As discussed by all the participants in Volume 3, the looting of the African continent for the interests of European capital accumulation resounds today in the rejection of any historical or moral obligation for the repatriation of stolen art objects. As Hartman describes, this points to the necessity of developing a more robust language for distinguishing between accumulative and non-accumulative activity:

We have a term for that [European, capitalist] kind of looting and it's called *accumulation* or conservation. So what does it mean to think about accumulation . . . in relation to looting or rioting . . . . *Where is the robust left analytic that extends this thought in deed?* We don't call accumulation looting or theft because we have other language for it: the historical conditions for the reproduction of capitalism. Without such an analytic, we continue to distinguish between these two orders—accumulation and looting—and treat them as if they aren't intimately entangled.[12]

Read in the context of the ongoing genocide in Gaza and this semiotic attack on Palestinian life, the urgency of constructing this "robust left analytic" for the social practices of looting and rioting equal in rigor to Marx's category of accumulation makes itself most urgently felt.[13] Writing in the immediate aftermath of the Arab defeat during the 1967 Arab-Israeli war, Tunisian revolutionary and former member of the Situationist International Mustapha Khayati emphasized that the "Palestinian question is too serious to be left to the states," since it remains "too close to the two basic questions of modern revolution—internationalism and the state."[14] Khayati's analysis remains correct regarding the organizational forms necessary for revolution and the social formations which will disappear (insofar as their existence depends upon the organic composition of the capitalist mode of production).

The struggle for Palestinian liberation is present across all three volumes. For Volume 1, the colors of the cover (pink, green, black), those of a watermelon, were chosen in solidarity with Palestinian resistance in 2021 to the eviction of families in Sheikh Jarrah. In Volume 2, the participants discuss how the question of support for Palestine caused rifts in migrant solidarity movements in Berlin. In all the volumes, we have worked towards a type of analytic described by Hartman, endeavoring to identify tactics, strategies, and practices that are non-accumulative processes of appropriation across various sectors of production, reproduction, and creativity. We hope that the collection of these conversations in one place will encourage further discussion and collaboration.

VOLUME 1

INSIDE AND OUTSIDE: INFRASTRUCTURES OF CRITIQUE

*Michael Rakowitz, Shellyne Rodriguez,
and Stevphen Shukaitis,
moderated by Andreas Petrossiants*

In 1957, in what would become the founding text of Situationism, Guy Debord wrote: "Something that changes our way of seeing the streets is more important than something that changes our way of seeing paintings."[1] On its face, this is an invitation to spend less time tinkering with the forms or modes of institutionalized aesthetic production, and to instead commit to engaging with the everyday—an engagement which for Kristin Ross offers a "vantage point for social analysis" and "a way to understand past and absolutely contemporary alienations at the same time as all the various attempts to overcome them."[2] A focus on the street, as Ross argues elsewhere, would be a fundamentally political act because it becomes part of the everyday: "Political emancipation means emancipation from politics as a specialized activity."[3] Or as Henri Lefebvre puts it, "Revolutionary events generally take place in the street. Doesn't this show that the disorder of the street engenders another kind of order?"[4] Reading Debord's claim today, with the experience of numerous political struggles that have taken the spaces of culture's production and exhibition as sites of antagonism (whether bringing the street into the gallery or vice versa), we propose to reinterpret this opening salvo as a call for the abandonment of the illusion of art's autonomy and to see the street and art as coterminous across what are only ostensibly disparate fields of action. Here we focus less on tactics for bringing the war home or to the museum or into the everyday, because we recognize that the war is already in all those places, which is where it must also be fought.

Following analyses which discredit the long-held notion that the surplus value produced by art relates only to financial surplus, and that reject the idea that art's exhibition or reproduction can operate outside of the conditions of racialized and gendered capitalist mode of production, we propose to examine how the illusory borders between the spaces of art and the street (or everyday) are maintained by even well-meaning discourse and art theory. Looking back to how "critical" or "political" European and US-American art since the 1960s through today has been historicized, we see that the gesture of (artistic) critique is thought to operate along one of two vectors.[5] Some commentators describe critique that goes "inside"—an institution, a system—in an effort to subvert or usurp its operating protocols, sometimes using that institution's platforms to disseminate critical pedagogy, like Hans Haacke's use of the exhibition format since 1971 to display research about the role of art sector elites in extractive and repressive activity. The other category collects gestures that go "outside," sometimes referred to as "dropping out," a form of anti-institutional refusal. Protest movements and militant struggles are often subsumed into this damaging historicizing framework in other disciplines as well—a reminder that sites for culture's reproduction can make wider forms of counterinsurgency and class segmentation more visible, not to mention that they act as sites for its implementation.

We have convened a series of conversations titled *Diversity of Aesthetics*—a phrase originally formulated by Nitasha Dhillon to repurpose the anarchist dictum "diversity of tactics" to think aesthetics from decolonial and abolitionist frameworks. Later, the phrase was described by a member of the International Imagination of Anti-National Anti-Imperialist Feelings as "a different way of living because it's about a different way of sensing the world . . . the way we talk to each other, the way we exchange posters or the way we make videos or the way we dance or think about our freedom is a complete reorientation away from what has been institutionalized." The motivation of this series is to discuss how to variously conceive of and actualize struggle against institutions without being subsumed into the frameworks of sanctioned critique, without acknowledging the validity of those inside/outside borders unless it is to our advantage. This is the first of those conversations. Here we have invited Michael Rakowitz, Shellyne Rodriguez, and Stevphen Shukaitis to consider, among other questions: how is it possible to enter or exit the space of the institution and act in such a way that cannot be recuperated—or wherein the recuperation is beneficial to abolition and political struggle? We discuss concrete social movements, actions, and coalitions that we have either participated in or observed, and through these case studies we examine art history and its contemporary constellations. The discussion is neither a movement text nor an art historical one. This is a provocation, like Debord's, that is rooted in our various experiences between publishing radical texts, teaching, creating and writing about art, contesting capitalism, racism, (neo)colonialism, and other forms of exploitation, and thinking about how those systems of violence are threaded through and use the art institution. We make references to recent cycles of struggle in the art world, including the Nine Weeks of Art + Action at the Whitney Museum of American Art in 2019 and the 2021 Strike MoMA initiative underway as we conceive of this project. We borrow from and expand upon a methodology proposed by Marina Vishmidt that she terms "infrastructural critique,"[6] which acts to bridge the connections between systems of repression and ideology on one hand, and culture, creativity, and artistic production on the other.

—Andreas Petrossiants and Jose Rosales,
May 2021

Andreas Petrossiants (AP) I thought it might be nice to introduce ourselves. Is that really corny?

Stevphen Shukaitis (SS) It's probably cringe, but it's also probably useful.

AP All right! Michael, want to start us off?

Michael Rakowitz (MR) Okay, well, I'm an artist and an educator living and working in Chicago. For a while now, I've been trying to figure out how to navigate the art world and to work with it. I feel especially committed to wielding the things that I found exciting about being an artist at first, while disrupting the norms. In the last few years, I've grown a lot more exhausted and a lot angrier at the way in which we pretend to be part of a radical imagination, when in fact, the art world has become part of the architecture that concretizes and extends systems of not just oppression but also boredom.

Shellyne Rodriguez (SR) I'm an artist. I have been a community organizer. I'm on unofficial retirement right now, but I organized in the Bronx with a group called Take Back the Bronx, and we've been kicking shit around here for the past ten years. I co-sign everything that Michael just said. But, I'm a bit more old school. I draw, I paint, I make sculptures. I'm a New Yorker, born and raised here. My parents are Puerto Rican and came here with their parents through Operation Bootstrap, that first migration wave post-World

War II. Apart from that, I'm somebody who managed to collage together some art degrees. With those degrees in hand, I began to step into a city that was violently against the people on the periphery, where I come from, so I ended up straddling these two worlds. The people from my hood are essentially treated as an expendable labor force that people in power have been trying to get rid of since the '60s, to replace them with knowledge workers. Ironically, I ended up becoming a knowledge worker myself. So, it's just a really interesting and isolating space to stand in. I find myself fighting with the art world more than participating in it. I'm like a persona non grata. We're definitely at a moment when we need to dismantle and rebuild across the board. The art institution is just a microcosm where we can begin all the dismantling and rebuilding.

SS My background is somewhat conflicted and confused. Imagine that you have a business card holder, but the two cards say completely different things. I grew up in Pennsylvania and came of age in the punk scene doing independent media production. I worked for a few record labels and WBAI Radio in New York. I dabbled in journalism and did that for some years, and then realized in the early 2000s that the culture industries were becoming really hard to make a living in. I wasn't sure what to do, so I thought I'd do a PhD. I couldn't get in anywhere and then, long story short, while working in Amsterdam I got an email saying "come to the University of Leicester School of Management, we have an anti-capitalist business school." So I ended up doing a PhD on collective forms of imagination, art, and autonomous politics. And, somehow, since then I've been working in the business school. Since 2004, I've balanced teaching with work for the publisher Autonomedia, and since 2009 that includes editing the Minor Compositions publication series. I've also worked on different art exhibitions. So I have the work that I want to be doing on the one side, and then there's the everyday work in a business school, which is kind of weird—things that don't fit together very well.

SR It's the nature of this shit. Nothing fits together very well, but here it is.

SS Right.

AP I was born and raised in Brooklyn. I lived in Italy for a few years and then wrote an MA in art history in London that sketched some connections between *operaista* (worker-ist) critiques of unions and political parties in the 1960s and 1970s and how they could be applied to the historical theo-rization of institutional critique. To pay the bills, I work as an editor.

I think those intros are so exemplary of why I was excited to speak with you all for this first volume. This conversa-tion builds from many others that I've had with friends and comrades over the last few years thinking about the notions of critique and struggle as they relate to the border sketched by the institution, and not just those in art (museums, gal-leries, and so on). That is, the supposed line demarcating the inside and the outside of some system or space of exhibition, representation, or repression. Historically, Euro-US philoso-phers of aesthetics argued that artistic work is "autonomous" from labor, meaning that it functions differently from other practices, work or leisure—or as my friend Marina Vishmidt says, art was presumed "autonomous" because it is dependent on financial surplus and not on labor. This helped justify nationalist expansion and colonial looting to fill the coffers of the state and its elites. Today, it's almost ironic that neo-liberal art institutions—as well as other nonprofits and for-profit institutions—have used this ideology to profess being "neutral" with regards to geopolitical violence and capitalist exploitation—a euphemism for profiting from culture while reproducing the systems of expansion and violence that are often being critiqued in the work they exhibit.[7]

The Rockefellers were terrified of Hans Haacke's *MoMA Poll* in 1970—a work in which he invited museumgoers to vote on whether "the fact that Governor Rockefeller has not denounced President Nixon's Indochina policy" would influence their vote in his reelection—to the point that the artist decided to covertly install it the day before the famous "Information" exhibition opened. Today, managers and board members might relish the exhibition of similar politically informed art as a way of pretending to be "allies" of antiwar sentiments while profiting from those wars, if it fits in the forms of presentation dictated by the museum. I'm thinking of something like MoMA PS1's recent show "Theater of Operations: The Gulf Wars 1991–2011," about the US wars in Iraq. The show professed a historical critique of the wars while MoMA's board member Leon Black profited off massacres of Iraqi civilians. And, as you might want to talk about later, Michael, the curators ignored your requests to adjust your work in response to information surfacing about MoMA's financial connections to violence in Iraq and, instead, gaslit you. Another recent example is the incongruence between PS1 doing a show on abolition and incarceration called "Marking Time: Art in the Age of Mass Incarceration" while another board member, Larry Fink, is one of the country's biggest profiteers of private prisons. I'd like to ask to start us off: how can one be critical of or antagonistic toward the institution, without handing over the self-determination of the work, whether it be art or grassroots organizing? In other words, how can we enter or exit the institution and act in such a way that our actions and production cannot be recuperated—or anticipate the recuperation and make it beneficial to abolition and struggle?

SR The first thing that came to mind, when you said artistic autonomy was presented by critics and theoreticians of modern art "as other" to labor—meaning that it functions differently from other practices—was Lucy Lippard's essay "The Pink Glass Swan." She argues that artists are literally one of the only types of workers who own the means of their production. She says: "For years now, with little effect, it has been pointed out to artists that the art-world superstructure cannot run without them. Art, after all, is the product on which all the money is made and the power based."[8] It just pisses me off a bit because Lucy wrote this in the '70s. It's kind of like a broken record, you know? Talk about gaslighting, right Michael?

MR Well, there's a larger program of gaslighting here with what you're bringing up Shellyne: the fact that people have to tell the same stories over and over and over again, they have to include their stories of having been oppressed or having been abused as part of this "diversity-equity-inclusion" industrial complex, but the institutions don't listen. Instead, this system essentially exhausts people to the point where they just can't relive these things anymore. Writing and statements about oppression have become so appropriated by the system that this kind of writing that did have an urgency has subsequently become anesthetized, which has led me to a point where I do have my doubts about institutional critique. And I say this with all the respect to our ancestors and our elders who have engaged in this practice. It wasn't easy work for Hans Haacke. It wasn't easy work for Mierle Laderman Ukeles. These artists were not using their projects to create another niche of marketable and identifiable work. But when it does become codified, you have to go back to that original anger that led us to a place like institutional critique and see where it can lead us now.

That's one of the reasons why I love the arguments in MTL+'s 2018 essay in *October*, "From Institutional Critique to Institutional Liberation," in which they argue that the stakes of critical work need to be higher.[9] The work needs to be something that can't be sold. It leads me to want to return artwork to a place where it never needed the museum, the institution, or the patron. And Shellyne, I'm so grateful that you brought up that Lippard essay because I first read that in the '90s when I was in school and working for an architecture group called SITE (Sculpture in the Environment). They're responsible for all those buildings for a company called Best designed to look like they were falling apart. They really took deconstruction to an illustrative and literal extreme. James

Wines of SITE wrote a book called *De-architecture*, where he talks about how earlier civilizations—and I refuse to use the word "ancient" because all it does is disconnect the people to whom the work belongs—like Greek, Egyptian, Babylonian, and Assyrian did not have separate words for art and architecture, which includes housing, civic spaces, and so on. So, I want to see culture start to seep back beyond the performativity of "art and life" and start to find its way into spaces that don't need patrons to launder their reputations. Into spaces where we do away with the belief that work needs to be cared for by a specific group of people who create structures that are *careless* of other people.

SS The discussion so far makes me think that we aren't necessarily inside or outside so much as we are constantly negotiating a set of ambivalent relationships with different institutions and their networks. So the question is how we negotiate them and what those negotiations produce. That could happen in a really crappy way like the "diversity-equity-inclusion" industrial complex, or it could happen through the process of going in and out or changing spaces to create other kinds of relationships in that negotiation. I'm thinking back to things like the original calls for art strikes in the 1970s, Gustav Metzger's in particular, in which he essentially says: stop making art, but don't stop making things all together. It's about going on strike to find time to create more collective resources.[10] It's about choosing how one is networked or connected, not to self-maximize or network one's way into places, but, rather, to ask: how can we use the energies of these connections to do something else? And I think that's important because I don't think there really is a space outside of recuperation. Anything outside of recuperation is actually outside of politics altogether. So it's how you negotiate the spaces and the connections you have.

AP Michael, I'm grateful that you mentioned Mierle Laderman Ukeles' work because her work is my go-to example for the way critical projects in the past have been recuperated fifty or so years on. I think one of the more important examples is her *Maintenance Art Manifesto* (1969) but not necessarily for the reasons that most people historicize it or celebrate it—though the whole thing is strikingly brilliant. And this is to your point about negotiating connections, Stevphen. She wrote the manifesto in 1969, in a fit of rage, after she was told by art school professors and other men that she couldn't make art as a mother, after the structural, patriarchal conditions made art production incredibly difficult while she was working in a factory and raising children. Most people make reference to the first section of the manifesto, in which she introduces the double-linguistic shift that would be the framework for much of her work: all her work is maintenance and all her maintenance is art, thus everything she does in the home, in the museum, and in between is maintenance, is art. Less remembered is the second part of the manifesto, which is an exhibition proposal to turn a museum into a waste management site, a way of using the institution's physical spaces to engage parts of the local, municipal, and spatial infrastructures of the city.

This was happening in the era when New York was descending into near bankruptcy. In 1976, financial elites and the federal government forced New York to sell off its relatively robust welfare structures, while extorting the mayor to lay off sanitation workers, close schools, implement tuition at previously free city colleges, close public hospitals in majority black and brown neighborhoods, and so on. The reason the city ran out of money was because major banks refused to buy city bonds and instead invested in other countries around the world. Kim Phillips-Fein's *Fear City* is a great historical recounting of this moment.[11] In any case, the reason I bring up this particular aspect of Mierle's work in historical context is to introduce the scene for her early workerist projects, produced as artworks, and how they have been eaten by the city's neoliberal city government and art world today.

The saddest example of such recuperation regards the project in which she became the artist in residence at the

Department of Sanitation in 1979. At the time, she got backlash from all sides. First of all, she was going into these giant sanitation centers, speaking with heavily exploited workers, and making documentary films in the spirit of productivist projects. In one instance, she documented how some two hundred or so workers had one barely functioning shower. She told me that one of the waste processing plants she walked into had one entire wall covered in porn. She would walk in and all the men would balk at her project, right? It wasn't the most welcoming environment for an "institutional critique" artist, particularly a woman. But, she was also getting critiqued by second-wave feminists who chastised her for working in and with an all-male institution—this very reductive feminism that labeled her "anti-woman" because she was interested in the class and racial oppression of a crucial municipal workforce—an extension, by the way, of the patriarchal-capitalist divisions of production and (social) reproduction, which she intimately understood if not in those terms. In short, Mierle risked and received critique from all sides—from other artists, from feminists, and from the workers themselves.

In the most tragic example to my mind, the city has coopted her original project. In the era of Mayor Bill de Blasio, the city created an "artist-in-residence" program using Ukeles' language, placing cultural workers in various city agencies. Except now, those positions serve to artwash over the administration's violence and economic borderline austerity. For example, Tania Bruguera was named the artist-in-residence for the New York City Mayor's Office of Immigrant Affairs—the same mayor's office that continued to evict undocumented workers while Immigrations and Customs Enforcement policed poor neighborhoods. But this process isn't specific to Bruguera. The point I'm making is about the repurposing of a historical project that *criticized* and *documented* the city's mistreatment of a crucial workforce into a decoration that sanitizes the city's image today.

SR One thing that comes to mind is my feeling that "art for art's sake"[12] did for the political potential of art what the single-issue "winnable demand" coined by Saul Alinsky—crystallized in the nonprofit industrial complex—has done to grassroots organizing.[13] The work of Bruguera, or other contemporary "socially engaged artists," or even as Michael said, that of our ancestors of institutional critique get sucked right in and absorbed, while communities like mine are turned into subject matter or even raw material for grant applications. The other way I'm thinking about the "inside/outside" thing is through my own experiences working at MoMA as a community access educator for eight years. So, the question: "how can one be critical of or antagonistic to the institution, without handing the self-determination of the work, whether it be art or grassroots organizing," makes me think of two things in the context of that job I had—at least, before I was fired along with the rest of the education staff during COVID-19 which was the year after the museum's multimillion-dollar expansion. On the one hand, what you get is a curatorial staff that believes in the work and the power of art to overcome structures of violence, but they refuse to admit that work can't redeem the institution, no matter how well-intentioned they are. So, if you're inside, you have to refuse to contend with the cost-benefit analysis. As long as these board members' wealth—that is generated via global, capitalist extraction—remains integral to the way that these museums function, then refusal is just a form of self-preservation, a fight against the systems that want to kill us.

On the other hand, I think about the historical function of the museum in European modernity and historical attempts to make those functions visible through art. I used to bring the kids I was teaching to see Marcel Duchamp's *Bicycle Wheel* (1913), the first readymade—the first instance of an artist producing an artwork by *selecting* a mass-produced object and placing it somewhere, rather than literally "creating" something from raw materials. But that discussion, the way the readymade is taught, is incomplete, right? For the readymade to become an artwork, as Duchamp would say later, you also need some institution (art history, the museum, and so on) to confirm that selection. So I'd try to explain to them how this became art. I'd tell everybody to walk out of the room, and I would take off my Adidas sneaker and set it on the floor, and when they came back in, I'd ask, "What's this?" And they're all trying to figure the Adidas out, and I'm like, "Bro, I'm literally not wearing a second shoe!" So, that's my way of showing how this space, the museum, creates a weird distance between the object and viewer. That Schopenhauer thing about how you pluck the "object of its contemplation" out and put it in a sacred space. There's this weird distance; whatever you put in there gets neutralized. Because it becomes something to contemplate and not something to act on. I think that the work MTL+ and Decolonize This Place (DTP) do is to eat that shit backwards, to recuperate back the recuperated.[14]

I also want to more precisely respond to the second part of your question: whether there is something that can be done from the inside? Well, I got a list here about what I did from the inside of MoMA: I stole as many art supplies as I could and gave them away; I painted banners for the Whitney protests[15] with their materials; I undermined the museum as much as I could; I used the galleries as a site for political education; I created a culture among my students and my audiences that set them against the institution but *in alliance* with the art; I treated the institution like any "bullshit job"—shout out to David Graeber—and maintained the posture of general disgruntledness; I encouraged the education staff, comprised exclusively of freelance contractors, to try and form a union, us against the boss, us against the institution. Sadly, I think there are a bunch of really intelligent people who can't help but conflate the museum and art, the institution and art, the gallery and art. We're so fucking disciplined, it's scary. And they fired me, so I don't care, you can write that shit down. They can kiss my ass.

SS Would you say your practice of using the space in the ways you described and trying to work within and against the space could be called "institutional critique?"

SR Nah! But listen, I love that shit. Hans Haacke did *Shapolsky et al* (1971).[16] That was about the Bronx, in part. I love that work, but it was a different time. I don't want to be in the institution talking shit about the institution. I just worked there. I saw myself as a janitor, you know? I don't think that you can change it from the inside. I don't believe in that. I think it's too fossilized.

SS When you say you see yourself as a janitor, at what point are you a janitor and at what point are you a maintenance artist?

SR Haha! Good question, but I wasn't making art; I was teaching. I wasn't making art while teaching or using my teaching as part of my art practice, or anything like that. I make drawings. When I'm sitting in my apartment making art, it's a personal, philosophical inquiry, an endeavor that has nothing to do with those motherfuckers. But, here's the other thing about that—all the little teenagers I taught think that if you're an artist, then you must know how to draw. The first thing they would ask me is, "Can you draw me something?" But I think that what makes a person an artist is the ability *to see in space.* Period. My friend Ruthie Wilson Gilmore and I talk about that all the time. She's a geographer and abolitionist, and she always says that artists, like geographers, see in space. We, artists, see a certain something as it transpires in space, and that is the power that we have that needs to be applied. That ability is where the praxis is. Make what you want to make: paintings, conceptual art, performance, whatever. You know, that's nice and beautiful and all that. Bake a cake too. But, the question that needs to be asked is how are you taking your profound ability to see something and apply it? That's the contribution to the collective labor of the farm. If we're all on the farm, how is my ability to see going to contribute so that we can all eat?

AP Not to harp on Ukeles' work, but I wanted to go back to the question Stevphen asked you Shellyne about when you're a janitor and when you're an artist. Ukeles made an elegant work called *I Make Maintenance Art One Hour Everyday* (1976) in which she asked low-paid cleaning staff in a large office skyscraper to consider one hour of their drudgery as art. Then, she would go around the building and take polaroid pictures of them while they were working. After the picture was printed, she'd ask whether the photo captured them laboring or making art. The great thing about the work is that, in addition to critiquing the nature of the valorization of labor-power under capitalism—that an artist makes this much, a manager makes this much, and a cleaner makes this much, or, more precisely, how much surplus is extracted by each specific labor agreement—the piece also made visible the otherwise invisibilized sanitation work in this massive office tower, without which nothing could be done. Like Haacke bringing his research into the museum in the form of an artwork, Ukeles presents a workerist argument about the valorization of labor, but by engaging with workers themselves. This reminds me of the big protests at Goldsmiths University in 2018 that fought (and won!) to bring all cleaning staff in-house. Part of the fight targeted the new Centre for Contemporary Art, where organizers hung a banner in front of the museum asking, "Who keeps the cube white?"

To be clear, I'm not interested in reinforcing this assumed existence of an inside/outside framework; I'm interested in understanding how the academy theorized critique, and then how that binary needs to be dealt with in artistic production and antagonism going forward—how to get ahead of it, in a way. I want to get beyond the way 1960s Euro-US art through today has been historicized.

To my mind, it's important to note that social movements or militant struggles, when historicized, are subsumed into this historicizing framework as well. This shows yet again that systems of counterinsurgency and exploitation often play out more visibly in cultural spaces, which is why we should be looking there in the first place. In other struggles outside of cultural production, the assumed binary can take other forms, e.g., "violent" versus "nonviolent" demonstrators. Academics like Judith Butler are key to reproducing this type of differentiation as evidenced by their arguments that movements like the Arab Spring in Egypt were "nonviolent," when, in fact, demonstrators burned down precincts and fought back against the police *in addition* to the examples Butler underlines of collective performance—cooking, occupying squares, and so on. So, I think the inside/outside binary operates similarly to how violence versus non-violence is used by power to divide social liberation movements. The reason I really like how DTP have done things is because they play with that boundary. I remember a DTP organizer saying something during the Whitney protests about how they chose to enter the museum because it was a safer space than the street—literally using the assumptions of autonomy, professed by the museum director himself, to the advantage of keeping demonstrators safer from the police.

SR Mierle's work always reminds me of the Garbage Offensive by the Young Lords in 1969. The Young Lords were the equivalent of the Black Panthers for the Puerto Rican community. But in New York City, and in East Harlem, specifically during the years of recession and almost bankruptcy as the sanitation department laid people off, sanitation workers protested by refusing to come pick up garbage. And so, the Young Lords went to the sanitation office and confiscated, or "expropriated," the brooms and went through the community collecting trash. *Abuelas* came outside with their brooms and joined in. They swept all the trash and piled a five-foot-high pile of garbage in the middle of Third Avenue and set that shit on fire. *Now* the sanitation department had to come get it, along with the fire department.

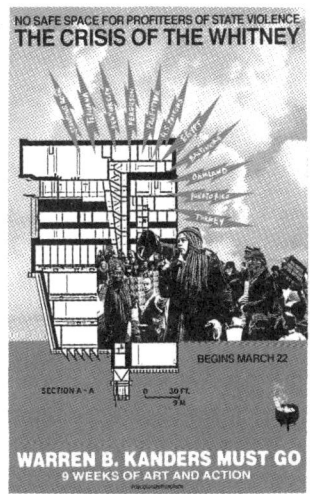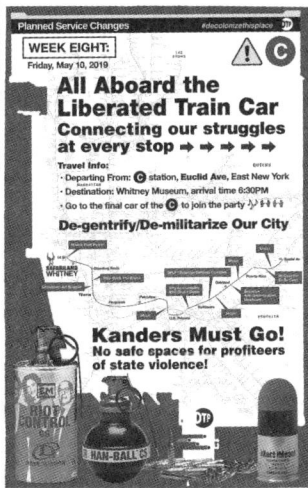

Posters produced by Decolonize This Place for Nine Weeks of Art + Action, New York City, 2019. Courtesy of Decolonize this Place.

MR I think we need new words. I love this conversation because it's like a tennis match, going back and forth and vacillating and being destabilized. That is essentially the soulful part of art as a critique where people don't have to come in with fluency in Marx or whatever else to recognize that spaces of leisure are increasingly disappearing, and that leisure is also increasingly shamed. Art is a shameful practice in so many ways and an elitist practice in so many ways as well. I think about Cao Fei and her work *Whose Utopia* (2006), a video piece for which people on assembly lines in China were given a day to make whatever they dreamed of making. It's this polished work that essentially builds on something that Mierle and her generation started. To take it in another direction, the artistic director of documenta 13, Carolyn Christov-Bakargiev, referred to all the people who participated in the exhibition as "participants" because all the artists were collaborating with non-art workers: architects, unconscious analysts, an assassin, and all these different occupations and roles. And she talked about her hope that the word "artist" would one day disappear because these creative kinds of moments would disperse into everyone's life to take it beyond the performativity of "everyone is an artist." I think that's part of what the "reciprocal readymade" that Duchamp proposed was getting at.[17] It was trying to give license to the absurdity of the Adidas in the white cube. But it also gets at the absurdity of most art museums today; they're fucking showrooms. Interventions like this get us thinking: what do we assign a value to, who's the author, why can't we see the author of the Adidas?

This is not a smooth segue but I want to go back to what you were saying, Stevphen, about Metzger and art strikes. I hoped that quarantine was going to be an art strike. And I think, in a lot of ways, maybe it has been. For example, Andreas and I are part of an effort that is going to one day produce an arts union, but a union that doesn't just sell out its members or other workers. But rather, something that plans to be part of the momentum of building power that is in line with what the affinity and working groups of Strike MoMA are doing.[18] This year, I've been thinking about my work as a compost. Not as something that I'm withholding necessarily, but, rather, considering how art can create nutrition and be used to grow more connections, more bonds, more relevant work. I'm really fascinated by your background Stevphen, talking about an anticapitalist business school, because one of the things that we're thinking about together in the Artists for a Post-MoMA Future Working Group—a group formed as part of the larger Strike MoMA initiative—is creating a kind of MoMA in exile, or a MoMA in waiting, and putting together a transition team. Shellyne, that's what you're talking about when you say being able to see something in space—that's the magic you know.

SR Andreas, you mentioned what DTP said about how the spaces of aesthetic autonomy can be safe places given that cops are less likely to enter them. When we were talking before about the white cube and how this neutralizing space turns around and eats our critique, I meant to signal that we need to think like that, in terms of guerrilla warfare tactics. It's like the Cu Chi tunnels in Vietnam. It's a reusing of those spaces. This was a museum—now it's a kitchen, a daycare center, an anticapitalist business school. And I think that's where the imagination needs to be. I think that the museum should be a public square, first and foremost, not just a mausoleum. So, let's make them public squares. But, because of the way that the Adidas lives in the space, or is defunctionalized in that space, that's where guerrilla tactics can come in. When the suspension happens, everybody has to think about what's being said, and then maybe the police won't rush in and crack your skull because the suspension of disbelief is happening. I think that's a smart way to use it against them.

AP In a previous conversation I had with Marina Vishmidt, we phrased that specific tactic like this: "The museum's aesthetic forms are not devalorized so much as re-tooled in the direction of abolition."[19]

SS There is definitely something important about guerrilla tactics. I don't want to go too much into the history of the business school because it's not terribly interesting, but the backstory of how you can even have something like "critical management studies" is useful. Part of why this happened is because in the 1980s Margaret Thatcher decided that she hated sociology, and so she defunded sociology departments in the UK. And then left-leaning Marxist sociologists suddenly discovered that they are "organization theorists" and started studying labor organization and moved over to business schools. It's sort of what David Harvey says: you don't solve the problem, you just move it around. That space closed and then it moved over into another space. If you can't do what you want to do there, then you move somewhere else. It reminds me of similar ideas from Fred Moten and Stefano Harney, whom I've worked with over recent years, when they talk about the undercommons as an exodus, but a type of exodus where you don't have to leave. So often there's something blocking you from doing what you want to do. For instance, they argue you can't study or experiment together in the university, so then you have to find somewhere else to do it. And if there are blockages to using the art space as a space of experimentation, then you have to move somewhere else. But the problem is that always moving in that way gets tiring.

Just to back up a second to your magical Adidas in the gallery, I'm also thinking about the interesting emerging court case between Nike and Lil Nas X and MSCHF, where Nike's lawyers are literally trying to prove that the sneaker Lil Nas X made is not art, that it's not parody, so that they can make the case that he's infringing on a trademark. If you have this whole history of the readymade turning things into art, now you have a counter-legal history of trying to prove that things are most definitely not art because then patents can be legally protected.

SR I absolutely love that situation. He literally remade a Nike. Like "fuck your trademark." It's beautiful. I laughed so hard. You know, I recently saw this video of Fred [Moten] talking and I think it really applies here. He says:

> The emergence of Black Studies in white universities is roughly coterminous with the moment at which I think we will be able to trace back to the beginnings of the liquidation of the university as an intellectual institution. The contradictions of the university as hedge fund, the university as real estate company, and the university as intellectual institutions, those contradictions are not sustainable. It doesn't mean that there can't be good work, or that there hasn't been good work done in Black Studies in universities. It just means we got to figure out an exit plan now. It could very well be the case that the real flourishing of Black Studies that everybody thought might have been occurring in the '80s or now, will occur when Black Studies makes its move away from the universities and back into our communities. And we should be preparing for that.

> We have to keep what has been given to us as gift and task,
> we have to keep that alive.

I feel like we can extend all these observations, predictions, and critiques that Fred is making to the art institution. Maybe artists and curators are so-called stewards of the practice and that is our task—like how you were describing it, Michael.

AP I want to connect the dots. First thing I'll say about this "participants" thing and about bringing together different types of production under the aegis of "creativity" that you brought up, Michael, is that, while it does certainly have a utopian or even emancipatory quality, under current regimes, I think it's also very dangerous to flatten "creativity" in that way under the rubric of "participating." Not that that was what Christov-Bakargiev was doing. I mean the way this "everything is art" message gets interpreted elsewhere and is happening on a massive scale with "creative capitalism." Marina has this great line about creativity under neoliberal capitalism. She writes: "Creativity functions as capitalist populism, assuring every exploited worker and discontented artist that capital's interests coincide with their own." So this can be damaging, but, as you're saying, Michael, it could also encourage a coming together as artists, but not under that label—but rather, as tenants, as workers, in cooperatives or even in libertarian municipalist organizations, for example. I'm thinking of something like the Rojava Film Commune here, a collective of filmmakers in the autonomous region of Rojava. The terms—artist, tenant, worker—aren't specific classes but, rather, forms of exploitation or forms of (re)production that can be overcome by creating solidarity networks across occupation, across fields, across income levels. The question is how to mediate between all those different positions at the same time.

A common enemy helps. I remember how incredibly wide the solidarity networks were that formed during the struggle against Amazon in New York City in 2018, when many different neighborhood groups came together to fight a proposed second headquarters. I think that to organize across different boundaries, we also need to understand how liberal counterinsurgency functions today. The second you criticize the museum from the so-called outside, people say, "Well, then where are we going to put the art? What are we going to do with it?"—implying that to antagonize and call for the dismantling of an institution's framework would also mean to call for the destruction of the tasks it fails to perform. This is similar to conservative retorts to demands for abolishing the police: "But who will keep us safe?"—as if the police make our cities any safer. Abolishing the police necessarily implies also thinking about community safety after the police are gone.

MR The first thing I'll say is a defense of Carolyn's utopian wish for the exceptionality of "the artist" as a term and subject position to disappear. I think Carolyn's vision makes it possible to move forward in a manner where we don't allow divide and conquer tactics to work on us—for instance, the way in which people and workers are treated at museums as opposed to the ways that artists are treated would no longer divide people in the same way in Carolyn's conception. The hands that make the work and the mind that thinks up the work are not mutually exclusive for me; they're not extractible positions. I want those relationships to remain intact. I want solidarity. I don't want museums to be able to reach out to artists and say something like, "These pesky art workers are protesting so we're going to increase the number of artists we have on our board," which is just a way of rearranging the furniture on the Titanic or engaging in a kind of illusion of a process. Many museum workers are also artists whose work we're not seeing in the museum because who gets shown has very little to do with questions about merit and quality. So, that's the kind of position from which I can see Carolyn's thought experiment extending what some Fluxus artists proposed, which is that everybody can be an artist and that everything can be art.

Boris Groys wrote this great text in *e-flux journal* called "On Art Activism" in 2014 that blew my mind, because he described the kind of work that I do, both artistically and on the street, let's say.[20] But what I didn't anticipate was that he was going to be able to bridge the work that I do on the streets with the work that I do in museums. He writes about how the museum is a space of definitive death. It has always been the place where relics are aestheticized, deprogrammed from their functions, and disconnected from the people that used them. He connects this to the reason that Russian leaders refuse to bury Lenin. Even though the public wants him buried, the government continues to let the corpse slowly rot in that box behind glass. The reason is that if Lenin's remains disappear from that vitrine, then Leninism could come back as a zombie.

The other thing I wanted to comment on is looting. When we think about the museum as a site that can and should be looted, there are also many ways to repatriate and restitute. Hakim Bishara interviewed me for a piece he wrote about the *Theater of Operations* exhibition at PS1,[21] which included eighty-two artists, thirty or so of whom were Iraqi. And I told him that essentially the MoMA had looted the MoMA. I told him that as far as I'm concerned, all that artwork in the show was being harmed by the curators and their refusal to even respond to our requests. Harm has nothing to do with relative humidity or temperature. Or think about the struggle at the Whitney in 2019. The museum staff wrote that brave letter about the tear gas canisters produced by the board member Warren Kanders' company, which are used in Palestine and on the US-Mexico border, and, at the time, the museum had a Warhol retrospective up. I've seen those tear gas canisters in Bethlehem in the artist Emily Jacir's garden.[22] The canisters are the same size as a Campbell's soup can. So now when I see a Campbell's soup can, I don't see the can or Warhol's appropriation of them anymore. I see the tear gas. A common response to the idea of repatriating looted works—like the responses to abolishing the police—is something like, "Who's going to be able to take care of it?" Enough with the fucking racism! Enough of the colonialist largesse. People know how to take care of shit. I think that we need to think about looting as something that can happen in reverse as an autonomous form of restitution because I'm tired of waiting and I'm tired of the bureaucracies that make it impossible. Right now, the Smithsonian is helping to rebuild the Mosul Museum. You know one of the terms that's in that contract? That the Mosul Museum can never ask for restitution of looted art from the Smithsonian's collection.

SR Wow. These motherfuckers know how to consolidate power.

MR When I hear "looting" it's like a trigger for me. I've grown up in a house where our entire identity was looted. I'm constantly doing the exhausting work of getting hate mail from Zionists who tell me there's no such thing as an Arab Jew, you know? I think that the anger that's emerging now in antiracist, anticolonial movements is a powerful engine. Love and rage are going to do a lot to save and restore these works.

SR Damn Michael, you just dropped the microphone.

AP What you're saying makes me think of that awesome tag coming out of Minneapolis last summer: "You've stolen more from us than we could ever loot."

SR You know, in the Bronx, we're getting a hip-hop museum. So, they're putting the Adidas behind the vitrine right now. I've been fighting gentrification since I came out of grad school and got slapped in the face with the fact that artwashing was literally the bulldozer for real estate development in my neighborhood, as elsewhere. So, the fact that the hip-hop museum has already broken ground and they have all the big names on the board is tragic to me. The Bronx is like the last place in the city that hasn't gone down. I often joke and tell folks that in the Bronx I can go months without

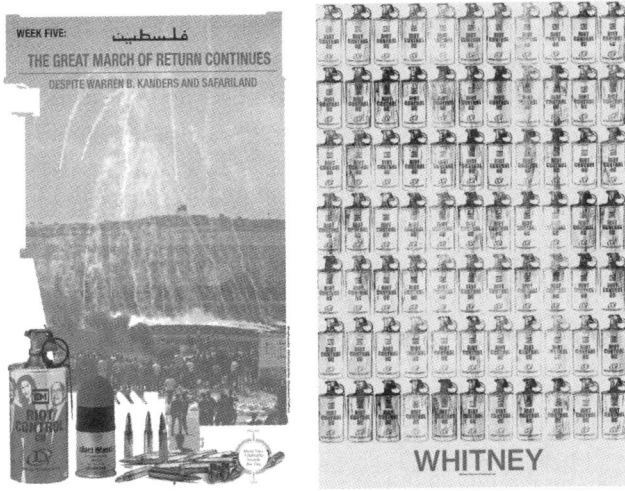

Posters produced by Decolonize This Place for Nine Weeks of Art + Action, New York City, 2019. Courtesy of Decolonize this Place.

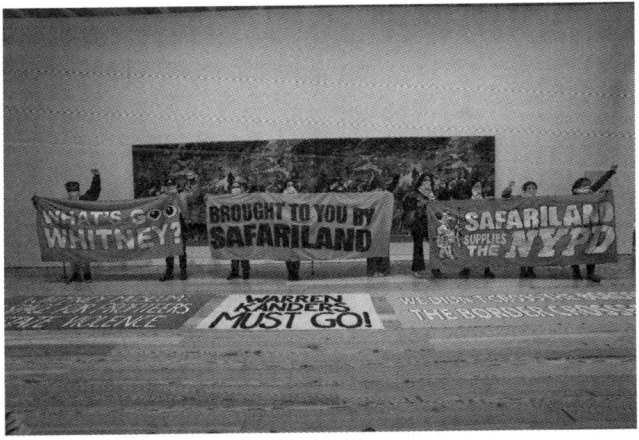

Demonstrators holding banners inside the Whitney Museum of American Art during the Nine Weeks of Art + Action, New York City, 2019. Photograph by Andres Rodríguez von Rabenau. Courtesy of Andres Rodríguez von Rabenau.

seeing a white person. So, this whole dilemma about "white people to the front" or "white people to the back" and similar liberal-minded arguments that take over protest movements in other parts of the city don't exist here, or at least not in that way. But, regardless, we're the poorest borough in the city, and one of the poorest counties in the country. I just can't shake the feeling that once they start to place all the Adidas sneakers behind vitrines, that will really be the nail in the coffin. Once they build a mausoleum, they can start to extract everything and place it in that grave—then they no longer need us around. I see the Bronx through Mosul right now, you know? And that leads me to the importance of internationalism between domestic colonials.

Michael, you nodded at issues of identity and the way that museums have weaponized that shit. I want to be flagrantly on record as saying that practically simultaneous with the success of removing Kanders from the board of the Whitney, the Brooklyn Museum was stacking its exhibition programming with black, queer, latinx shows—literally stacking the bodies of black, brown, Indigenous, and queer people, one after the other after the other. The Metropolitan Museum of Art had Wangechi Mutu statues in their fucking arches. And Kehinde Wiley had that confederate statue in the middle of Times Square, with a black man instead of a white man. The museum and the city are using work by artists of color as a literal front line to protect themselves. Listen, white supremacy hasn't needed white people for a long fucking time, and that's not my line. Lorraine O'Grady made that point at the Brooklyn Museum a couple of years ago in conversation with Aruna D'Souza. White supremacy doesn't need white people. This is Fanon 101. In order to keep power, they will give you a multicultural imperialism. So, I don't care what your identity is. I want to know what your politics are. The only reason people come to New York City is for upward mobility, but some of us have already been here. Our grandparents came here to work in factories when there was still that kind of work, and now we're here by default.

But yeah, the line in the sand is: where are your politics? I don't care how you identify. And as you all know, that kind of framework produces cognitive dissonance and cosmetic radicalism. Or to put it differently, we have to ask: what are the ends and goals of our struggles? To subvert something is not the end; it's the means to the end. The end is dismantling empire. Your politics don't begin and end with "Black Lives Matter"—they're supposed to end with the dismantling of white supremacy, the police, houselessness, empire. If racial capitalism is what the fuck it is, then we understand that the movement of capital is what subjugates and we need to stop it. Park your ass in the space and stop the movement of capital. I'm mad about that Mosul shit, Michael.

AP Now you dropped the mic.

SS There was one thing I wanted to say about an earlier point, but I've been holding off on it, because I don't have anything of equal mic-dropping intensity. I've been thinking and reading about artwashing a lot, and it struck me that there's a point made in many conversations on artwashing that gets it wrong. There has always been this assumption that the function of artwashing is to influence the general public or a wide audience. The assumption is that if some company sponsors an exhibition at a museum, then people will be more inclined to view the company differently. But I think that gets it wrong. I've been reading through histories of boycotts, in particular boycotts of Nike in the '90s that targeted the company for sweatshop labor. One of the interesting things that happened is that, while boycotting did make a temporary dip in Nike's sales, in the long run it didn't actually affect them that much. The sales dips are not what caused them to change their behavior. What eventually got them to respond was that they couldn't hire designers. They couldn't hire artists to work for them. What freaked Nike out wasn't that people stopped buying Nikes, but, rather, that their reputation was tarnished among prospective creative workers. Similarly, what happens with artwashing in the museum is not a company trying to impress its public by sponsoring MoMA or the Tate or whatever. Rather, they're engaged in a much more specific and targeted operation trying to get their employees to feel a little bit better about themselves, trying to get their employees to say that it's okay to work for this crappy arms manufacturer or crappy oil producer or whatever, because they're also doing this nice thing on the side. Artwashing does function as a sort of psychological reputation management operation, but it's not one focused on the general public. It's focused on a much smaller segment of workers or prospective future employees. If you think about artwashing in these terms, it becomes much easier to link this process to a labor discourse. With that knowledge of who the true targets of the washing are, you can create different lines of alliance and different tactics to sabotage those work practices.

AP That's super interesting. I agree that it's important to be specific about how artwashing works, and through what channels, but, since I do think it functions in a few ways, we should be aware of all of them. On the one hand, there's the very tangible way that artwashing happens, which Shellyne describes in her killer essay "How the Bronx was Branded."[23] Shellyne, you write about a very specific initiative in the Bronx that included rappers like Swizz Beats, giant real estate developers, and the police rushing into a community to organize concerts, studio residencies, and so on, all to prime an area for luxury real-estate development. The examples are unbelievable. You talk about a party that a developer organized that had flaming cars in it as decoration, referring to rampant instances of landlords burning down the homes of black people to claim insurance money after the land lost value in the '80s. What the fuck?! That's the material, visible, street-level way that art is used to wash images and processes of displacement and violence. It's also how greenwashing functions in contemporary cities. Build a park, make it nice, then kick everyone out. But then there are two other broad functions of artwashing: sanitizing the image of a company—including the way Stevphen talked about—and sanitizing the money itself. The latter has to do with the more boring accounting of it—the museum, like all other nonprofit institutions, at least in the US, takes dirty money and makes it tax-deductible.

SR That's really sharp. In New York, we've been trying to get knowledge workers to stop being wet noodles for some time, but upward mobility is a hell of a drug. The thing about culture is that it's a gift and a curse. It can be a weapon for liberation, and the next minute it can be weaponized against you. In the case of New York, the museums have become hot spots and hubs, a kind of psychogeography for the type of people I call the "neoliberal migrants" who come to New York. They come here, they want to party, see art, be in the scene. The museum becomes the content provider for all those things. Then you get big-time developers on the board of trustees. It becomes this ring structure, with the museum at the center. So, to my mind, the connections between corporations and art institutions are less about targeting the perspectives of workers these days and more about moving real estate. You get the executive directors in the first ring, and the rank and file in subsequent rings, and then, in the very last ring there's the people who deliver your takeout and drive your Uber, living in the outskirts, when they used to live right here. The museum starts to perform the functions of displacement and development. And it's been in that role since the neoliberal turn.

How can we flip that shit and make the museum a public square that's in our control? That process inevitably brings the people antagonizing those spaces into tension with the yet-to-be politicized neoliberal migrants who participate in that lifestyle culture while perhaps "critiquing" it, going to marches, etc. This confrontation produces a re-negotiation between the neoliberal migrants and the underclass that could, at its best, produce new vectors of solidarity. Part of the problem in New York is that people don't want to admit that they want the money and to be a part of the thing.

MR Yeah, I agree with everything that you just said Shellyne, and Stevphen, I appreciate the analysis of how to dive deeper into what artwashing means. I've always understood art-washing as something that allowed the nation states that these companies operate in to feel better about their operations in the world. The very building that I'm in right now, my office at Northwestern University, is tied to the Crown Family who are on the board of the university. The wealth of their company, General Dynamics, is built on weapons production, white supremacy, the occupation of Palestine, the bombing of Iraqis. I think that the function of what Stevphen described—when the company can't hire people at a certain point—shows the potential impacts of boycott. That's what I hope to see in in Israel: a continued resilience of BDS (Boycott, Divestment, and Sanctions) and the Palestinian academic and cultural boycott, to produce a situation where artists will not show, where people will not play concerts there, in order to create a kind of fast, to use biblical terms, a desertification of culture. That's the point where you start to see potential breakages. All I know is that there are pressures that we can exert. Sculpture is the practice of the exertion of pressure, right? I was trained as a stone carver, and it was always about the removal of material, getting at that Michelangelo myth that, while carving the figure, he was "liberating" it. But if we think about the subtractive process of carving and see our work as the removal of ourselves, our own divestment, then maybe we get to a more liberated moment.

AP That definition of boycott is well put. I'm also thinking about "leverage" here in those terms, but beyond just refusal, too. One question that pops up whenever artists get together to organize is, "What leverage do we have?" But, in the factory for example, the leverage isn't necessarily just in (stopping) production—as in going on strike, right? Factory workers or artists should produce whatever the hell they want to produce or whatever they need, and outside of the constraints of the wage, the working day, and so on. The leverage is also in what we do with what has been produced, and the labor-power that produced it. In Mario Tronti's 1965 text "Strategy of Refusal," he describes how the working class is simultaneously the *articulation* and *dissolution* of capital, writing: "The working class cannot constitute itself as a party within capitalist society without preventing capitalist society from functioning. As long as capitalism does continue to function, the working class party cannot be said to exist."[24] Meaning, that for workers' power to come into being, they need to exit from the social relations of production that produce surplus value, which includes being a worker. My collaborator on this project, Jose Rosales, brought up Tronti's response in 2012 to the question, "Can you really be outside?":

> Can you really be outside? This is the question. I answer: yes. I am. I feel I am. For sensibility, even before for reason. This world, as it is, as it is historically organized and dominated, does not belong to me, it is not part of me, and therefore it is extraneous to me. I do not stop here. The fact is: I find, before me, a form of being in the world, which is also not metaphysical but historically determined, which demands and obtains a hostile relationship. This way of being, or this world of being, fights me, and I fight it. I am not subjected to the forms of struggle, I choose them: naturally as far as possible.[25]

The whole premise for him to be "outside" is by being constantly antagonistic to the world that he finds himself in, or as he phrased it elsewhere, being "within and against," which I think goes along really well with what you were saying, Shellyne.

I would go further to say that Tronti's line is a clear indictment of forms like the union or the political party—or perhaps the modern museum. Think about what happened recently at the Amazon union struggle in Bessemer, Alabama. After the defeat of the effort, Vicky Osterweil (who is collaborating on this project) wrote on Twitter: "[I] hope the lesson from the Amazon vote is [that] organizing toward a legal union vote isn't the path toward change and we need a bottom-up movement of action, sabotage, and strike." I would add that, while the union form might be obsolete, the act of unionizing certainly is not. What people do to build a union—the acts of coming together, sharing concerns, building worker power—are crucial to liberation. It's just that the union shouldn't be the end goal, as Shellyne was saying earlier. Once a union of cultural workers forms, why not use that bloc to then deal with the gentrification maintained by the museum, or fight along with the cleaners of the space who are not legally allowed into the same union? Could artists, or cultural workers broadly considered, be thought in the same light as how Tronti discusses the industrial worker? How can strategies like boycott, sabotage, and strike play out in the spaces of art?

SR I agree 100 percent that the strike is in perpetuity. I think you never really get out of the strike. What comes to mind is historian Robin D. G. Kelley's critique of afropessimism. He says, if you want to talk about the Black Radical Tradition, then you need to understand that this tradition maintains that we never lose. We ain't losing. The problem is that we're always winning, and our enemies just keep reconfiguring the power structure through reaction. They're reacting to the fact that we just refuse to die. It's not that "we are death," but, rather, we are living, and we refuse to die, and we continue to pivot. I think what I was saying before lends itself to that: stopping the flow of capital. When I read the Tronti quote, I was like, yes, large unions have already been sucked into systems of oppression and hierarchy—the pensions of unions are being invested to keep jails open. Any kind of strike must be wildcat, rank and file, and it needs to be dumping the manure in the fucking highway until we can figure out how to rebuild. Then that's the other question, related to what Michael was saying earlier, maybe we need new words, new language. Is "union" the right word, for example? And we have to figure all this shit out quick because now we're also trying to outrun the destruction of the planet.

MR Yeah, I think that maybe "bloc" might be a better word for organizing labor, you know? Like the "artists' bloc" as opposed to the artists' union, for example. A bloc/k can allude to a commons, to the street, to being out with your neighbors. But it can also be a blockage; it can be a clot; it can be the kind of thing that disrupts and stops circulation.

One of the things that I think is deflating is when you realize that there are people who privately support struggles against these museums but won't say anything publicly. That fear is something that we need to recognize as the material that needs to be carved and worked through. How to create the conditions for strike? Going back to what Stevphen talked about with Metzger, what does work stoppage look like? We didn't see it happen at the Whitney, did we? There was one moment when the boulder got over the hump—when artists withdrew from the show—but what's the epilogue to that? So you throw a wrench in the works—maybe Gulf Labor Coalition really did slow down the construction of the Guggenheim Abu Dhabi, which was being built with what is practically slave labor—but how do you throw the wrench into the system permanently, to not just delay but to stop it outright? So that it's not just about the Whitney, MoMA, or Guggenheim Abu Dhabi? What if we took that momentum from one group and applied it to every other museum that's expanding in the world, that's displacing communities in New York? Stevphen, what do you think? Is that something that could start to shake things up in a way, where it's not just symbolic and not just about constant petitioning?

SS I honestly don't know, but I would certainly like to see it happen. I've always been most interested in artists who are not just making stuff I really like, but artists who experiment with collective forms and cooperate together in producing the work. I'm thinking about groups like Just Seeds, the printmaking cooperative. They don't just make cool stuff;

they have also made their working process and distribution operations cooperative. For me, that sort of cooperativization of the way they produce and distribute the materials is a key part of the work as much as the content. I spend a lot of time listening to free jazz and experimental music. I like people like Peter Brötzmann and Ken Vandermark. I'm also a big fan of Catalytic Sound, based in Chicago, who made this cooperative in which thirty or forty different improv, free jazz musicians are working together to socialize their structures of producing and distributing music. They're experimenting with how they make music in the immediate sense, but also in how they record, how they distribute. It's like socializing the production process at a bigger scale. Those kinds of examples are super interesting and inspiring but not exactly the end goal in themselves—just as the union isn't the end goal, but that all the social relations created working towards the union are the best part. The cooperative isn't the end goal, but the things you create while you make it are really useful. It's like that horribly cheesy but still nice Eduardo Galeano quote about utopia being the horizon you walk towards.

MR Maybe the real friends are the ones we made along the way.

[*Everyone laughs.*]

SR If I can jump in, I wanted to say that Michael, bro, I'm just really sorry that you took all those Ls by being the first person to withdraw from the Whitney Biennial. They really fucking beat you down. They beat me down towards the end too. You were talking about the fear that makes people support quietly but remain silent in the public eye and seeing this fear has made me bitter. This endless number of congratulatory "right on" messages in my inbox, meanwhile we're like, "Come out to the museum," and . . . crickets. There's such a culture of clamoring for "civic responsibility" and "rights"—pink pussy hat with a

BLM shirt. But they don't recognize that their own fear isn't freedom. That it's authoritarian. They don't recognize the fascism in their fear of the repercussions for their career.

I worked at MoMA at the time when the abolition show was going up. I worked there with a lot of the youth from Passages Academy, which is like the education wing of the juvenile detention structure in New York City. So I was working with incarcerated minors all the time. My very well-meaning, liberal supervisor thought it would be a brilliant idea, knowing my politics, for me to sit in on some sort of advisory committee for the abolition show. This was around the time that folks were rallying to get Larry Fink, who profits from private prisons, off the board, and I didn't want to help with their show about incarceration. So I refused to be on the committee, and when I spoke with Nicole Fleetwood, the curator of the show about it, her first response was, "But you already work here." And that's the fucking problem! I work here because I pay my bills like this. I'm not a representative of this entity. And I'm not going to do the intellectual work of propping up their show. The idea that our complicity robs us of the ability to say anything is bullshit. It is literally fucking bullshit. You can bite the hand that feeds you. In fact, you *must* bite the hand that feeds you. Are we all okay with normalizing McCarthyism? Is our complicity an extension of white liberal guilt? No! You're supposed to say something anyway. You have to show up to the employee cafeteria and look at your boss like, "Yeah, that was me outside, how's your day today?"

AP There's this amazing quote from Tai Shani, who writes: "We should not be worrying about biting the hand that feeds us . . . . We should eat the hand, for it is . . . much, much tastier than the boot."[26] You know, we're constantly being fed by a hand. I use money and have a bank account—that doesn't mean that I support those structures of extraction and subsumption and theft, you know? So if I send money via PayPal to a bail fund in Minnesota does that mean that I'm supporting PayPal and Elon Musk?

MR Nope, absolutely not! And that is where we need to start to pull apart these terms like "institutional critique" and whatever else. In the Strike MoMA document: "Framework and Terms of Struggle," point five speaks to just this. It's about getting rid of this fear of not being "pure," as if our movements can ever be pure. It says:

> No one is pure in a colonized world. We all live by our contradictions. Working at MoMA and disgusted with MoMA? Being an artist and hating the art system? Teaching at a university and wanting to tear it all down? Studying freedom in college while you go deeper into debt? Struggling to pay rent but displacing someone else? A Ford Fellow who protests the Ford Foundation? Oppressed but also contributing to the oppression of others? This is the entangled dystopia of our present. We can see contradictions as impediments and be consumed by frustration, ambivalence, and despair, or we can acknowledge and heighten them. Quiet forms of subversion, deep conversations, mobilizations, large and small: each act we take further undermines the principles that sustain MoMA.[27]

Just because all of us have day jobs does not negate us working for a better day, you know? That kind of accusation that "you already work here" is the most unbelievable thing that I have had thrown back at me as well—it's like, okay, then I guess why not engage in child sacrifice? I've always wanted to know what my calf muscle tastes like, so maybe I should just start self-cannibalizing . . . . It's criticism like this that's basically defeatist liberalism that makes one think, "Well just fuck it all." That way of thinking, that's the trap.

AP During the nine weeks of art and action at the Whitney, one night was about the US colonization of Puerto Rico. There were speakers and music in the museum lobby. One of the people speaking, a Mexican woman artist, was like, "I'm an American artist, but my art isn't in this American Museum of Art." And then she pointed the crowd's attention towards a Whitney worker who was filming the occupation and demonstration. She said that while her work isn't in the museum, some years from now that video of the protest would be shown in some exhibition about protest and institutional critique. I think this is a great demonstration of how the museum recuperates work. The readymade, for example, was partially about the artist "nominalizing" anything as art, because the artist's choice is part of artistic practice. But, as Duchamp alluded already in his "The Creative Act" (1957), "posterity" (acting through art's institutions) subsumes the function of the viewer, in part. Posterity decides who is remembered and who isn't. So, the museum (and the academy and so on) can nominalize what is and what is not art, *and*, also what is and is not protest, or critique. But what they cannot nominalize is *struggle*. That is the difference between critique and struggle. One is in the domain of the academy, or the museum, and one is in the domain of the street. And, I think, Michael, if you're comfortable to talk about them, your actions at MoMA PS1 in protest of the "Theater of Operations" show address this dilemma of recuperation quite well. Your planned action at the museum reminded me a lot of how the Greek artist Takis protested the inclusion of his work in the 1969 MoMA show "The Machine at the End of the Technological Era." He came in and literally removed his own work with his two hands. That action was what kicked off the formation of the Art Workers Coalition.

MR Well, I think what that experience at PS1 showed me was that even institutional critique is no longer tolerated. Initially when I was alerted to the connections between MoMA and US-backed killing in Iraq, I was willing to keep my work in the show for the connections it could produce with other works, and, also, for the historical potential that institutional critique might still have had. That said, I have a lot of gratitude to Phil Collins for withdrawing from the exhibition before it opened. For me, his work, *baghdad screentests* (2002) did the same thing that Jimi Hendrix's "Star

Spangled Banner" did at Woodstock. In the work, Phil films Iraqis, riffing on Warhol's screen tests. Because it's one of the most important works to be done about Iraq, the exhibition lost its anchor. And that set off a chain reaction for a lot of us, like Rijin Sahakian and Jananne Al-Ani. So, we went into the museum.

I wanted to put up a statement next to my work and pause the video. Not to withdraw, but to change my own work, *RETURN* (2004–present). Since the work was ongoing anyway and changes in response to the situation in Iraq, the work was not finished. But they rejected my proposals three times to put up the statement and pause the work. And I'm an artist who lives in the US, but there were two artists who live in Iraq in the exhibition, Ali Eyal and Ali Yass, who both had their interventions completely negated by MoMA PS1 as well. Ali Yass wanted to have his drawings slightly torn at the very end of the exhibition to show that he was in solidarity with MoMA Divest. His drawings were doubles of drawings that had burned when the Americans bombed Iraq. And when the museum caught wind of this plan, they *took down his work*. I mean, that is so fucking insulting. I realized that the days of *Shapolsky et al* are over. It's actually gotten worse. MoMA PS1, that institution where Gordon Matta-Clark carved up the floors, and Pipilotti Rist installed a video underneath the floorboards, doesn't exist anymore. The way that the museum operated, without ever commenting, is similar to how authoritarian regimes operate.

Let's look at that show as a case study for the history of institutional critique. Another case study that we need to be mindful of is the fate of the artist-research nonprofit Forensic Architecture. For the Whitney Biennial, they did something that isn't so rare or exotic. They made a video work about the chairman of the board, Warren Kanders, who we were all trying to get removed. But the result is that a Nazi hunter [Neal Sher, US Justice Department's Nazi prosecution unit] opened a lawsuit against them, because he thinks that they were using their platform and the Biennial as propaganda, and a nonprofit cannot engage in propaganda.

SR Thank you for that, Michael. I had no idea that PS1 was pulling that kind of stuff. That was one of the last shows that was up while I still had a job there. I created this night school or night studio for GED students in New York, where we would go to the museum, and we were at PS1 at the time that that show was up. PS1 tried to get around criticism by saying that it's not the same board as MoMA—they try to bob and weave like that. We know, though, that even with a storied past, how it begins is not how it ends. We know this when we think about the "progressive" nonprofits that are killing us right now. A lot of those NGOs and nonprofits that are now undermining real grassroots radical work by taking concessions and throwing others under the bus had radical, amazing beginnings. I want to think about this idea about bobbing and weaving, because in my own artistic practice I think in terms of syncretism, like *capoeira*, you know? The fight in the dance. The only way that we've ever been able to survive is by remaining unseen to some degree, hiding our *orishas* in Catholic saints. I think Stevphen was saying something to that effect about his work with Fred and Stefano, about the undercommons, the fugitivity, the outrunning. When we go back to what Andreas was talking about—that person documenting the Whitney protest—I think about how to outrun that recuperation, since it's guaranteed that they will flip everything, including your critique.

MR You know, when Stevphen was talking about the way people work together, those collaborations you mentioned, it makes me so excited about being together today to think about the ways that we can say these things in a room full of artists. One of the things that went out during week three of Strike MoMA from the Artists for a Post-MoMA Future Working Group was a call for an indeterminate and ongoing charrette to imagine a post-MoMA future—to think about everything from visionary architectural drawings and models and so on. In the text, we reference Yoshio Taniguchi, the architect who renovated MoMA in 2004 and who said: "The model for MoMA is Manhattan itself. The Sculpture

Garden is Central Park, and around it is a city with buildings of various functions and purposes. MoMA is a microcosm of Manhattan."[28] And, well, that's the problem! Because those neighborhoods have become exclusive places that have been exploited, extracted, expropriated, and so when we start to think about what that museum can be, we also have to think about what kind of city we want to live in. It might mean leaving it behind. I do a lot of cooking in my work and one of the questions I get all the time is: "Oh, you used to work with architecture, why are you suddenly cooking?" Well, Michael Pollan writes in his 2005 book *The Omnivore's Dilemma* that cities formed when people decided to cook together. If we can go back to that early scene, which explains why we want to be together in the first place, we can think about how we want our cultural objects to be treated and cared for. I'm really grateful for *this*, that we can think together instead of thinking with the gatekeepers.

SR Right on, Michael. I think Michael dropped the mic one last time.

AP Where do you get all these mics, Michael?

MR Michael's!

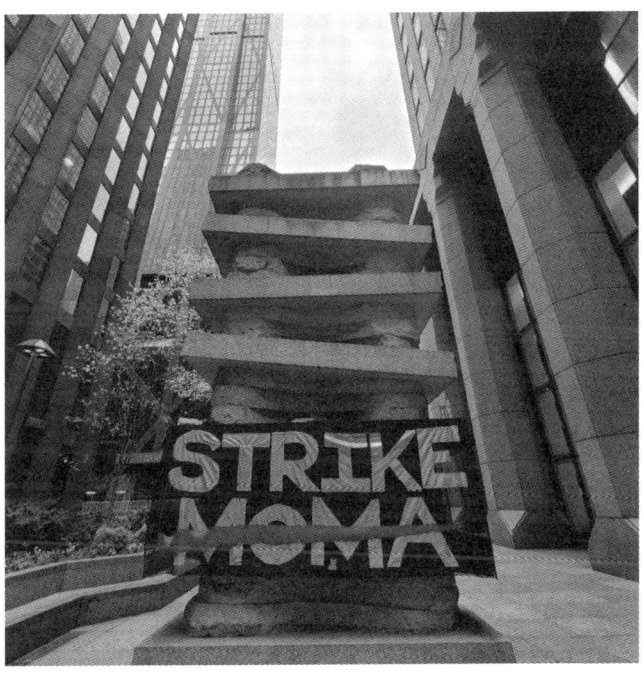

Banner by Strike MoMA hanging in Post-MoMA Plaza, New York City, April 2021. Courtesy of Strike MoMA.

FOREIGNERS EVERYWHERE

Claire Fontaine and Iman Ganji,
moderated by Jose Rosales

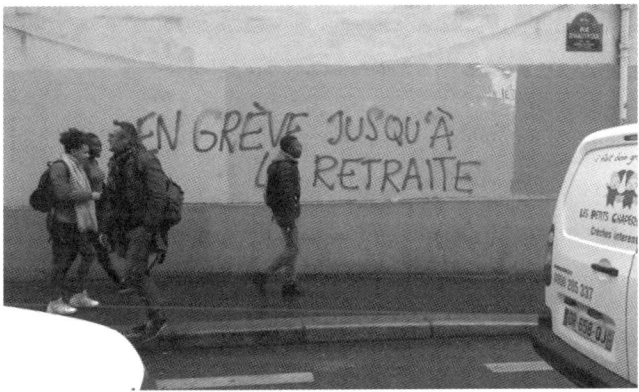

The following conversation with Claire Fontaine, Iman Ganji, and Jose Rosales was convened around two of Claire Fontaine's formulations: "human strike" and "foreigners everywhere." Over the course of the conversation, this exchange between comrades became a way of taking stock of the current conjuncture as it is shaped by innovations in the use and organization of strikes in the Global South (such as those of striking oil workers in Iran) and of the struggles of migrants and refugees in a world that has rediscovered the fascism at its heart. For the struggles born after the 2008 financial crisis, the riot seems to have assumed the role of the leading tactic at the cutting edges of the struggle against capital. This, however, is not to the detriment of the strike: *the riot does not signal the strike's retirement any more than paid leave or pension schemes free us from work.* Due to the university and the museum's monopoly regarding the reception of the human strike—i.e., the reception of a slow and thankless labor of renewing the strike-tactic outside of the point of production—this conversation belongs to an altogether other reception, where strikes become the collective practice of dis-identifying with that which makes us accomplices of power. This refusal to be an accomplice is what is at stake in Walter Benjamin's dictum, "to side with the proletariat is to become a foreigner in one's own country." From the wave of feminist strikes, as seen in the militancy of Argentine comrades, to Iman Ganji's Farsi translations of Claire Fontaine's writings and the ongoing strikes in Iran, where workers labor without a wage, bosses go without profits, and history continues without a single achievement—it is here that the strike begins to speak in a language foreign to previous cycles of struggle. We follow Verónica Gago and Marta Malo who describe this form of strike as:

> a political process [that] provides a common horizon of organization and practical investigation about forms of life and exploitation in specific territories while it also enables a continuous multiplication of the assembly form that becomes transversal . . . . The movement proceeds by constantly posing questions—What does your strike consist of? What is your struggle? What do we do? What do we *not* do?—that lead to an unprecedented level of communication expressed through war cries, chants, and actions that become tactical 'passwords' which are appropriated, replicated, and reinvented everywhere.[1]

The conversation has been collectively edited for clarity.

—Jose Rosales and Andreas Petrossiants
October 2021

A strike is an event which speaks and which is spoken about. It is a subject which loose[n]s tongues and makes ink flow freely . . . demands, protests, petitions, graffiti, discussions, harangues, slogans, shouts, cheers and insults are so many links in a chain of discourse that can give us a great deal of information about the aspirations, desires and conceptions of the workers . . . These are precious, fleeting forms, the skeleton of a movement in which too often we know only the principal actors. Silent sufferings, desires buried beneath the exhausting monotony of everyday life, rise up here and find expression.

—Michelle Perrot[2]

Jose Rosales (JR) One thing we enjoyed with the first volume was allowing everyone to introduce themselves. I can start us off. My parents left the Philippines in the 1980s because of the dictatorship. Despite my father's stint as a member of a union in the Philippines, I was raised in a very conservative environment. During undergrad I became friends with future comrades who would go on to form some very militant and refreshing groups. This period of "finding one another" culminated in our participation in the wave of UC occupations of 2009 and 2010.[3] This was a period when comrades from before and after the university occupation movement began to seriously reread Marx, Bataille, Deleuze, Foucault, Agamben, Tiqqun, and the at-times incongruous body of work that would form the reception of what is now simply called "communization theory" in North America.[4] Since then, I have involved myself in various, and at times transient, formations engaging in militant research wherever I am. I met Iman in Berlin, which was one of those rare encounters of meeting someone and feeling as if you've been friends your whole life; "we were [already] friends and did not know it."[5]

Iman Ganji (IG) I was born in Mashhad—the second biggest, but holiest, city in Iran. When I was eighteen years old,

I moved to Tehran. Later, some friends and I formed an autonomous leftist collective that was known by our website names: Schizocult and Schizofactory, both of which are now closed. When I was already out of Iran, we formed another website.[6] We identified ourselves as communists [*laughs*]. Then the Green Movement happened, followed by persecution. The state shut down our website, and I had to leave the country, even though I was not really one of the hardcore activists.[7] I mostly organized students and staged occupations in universities. Now I'm living in exile in Berlin and continue to keep open lines of communication between comrades in Europe and in Iran, which has been difficult. Iran is a very special mess. So, I am part of the diasporic, left opposition against the Islamic Republic and we continue our work outside Iran.[8] Here in Europe we also organize around issues to do with immigrants, anti-imperialist struggles, and, of course, Palestine. I also had a performance collective in Berlin but it's been about two and a half years since we've been able to produce anything.

JR You're being humble to a fault. Every comrade that I've met that is part of the Iranian diaspora knows you—if not by acquaintance, then from your numerous Farsi translations. During these early years, you helped translate eighteen books in total! And that includes texts by Claire Fontaine, Deleuze and Guattari's *A Thousand Plateaus*, Blanchot's *Political Writings*, Negri, Bataille, Agamben, Hito Steyerl, Gerald Raunig, and so on.

IG Yes, I did a lot of translating because I was part of a collective that worked to make these texts available online, and sometimes we published them as books as well. We put out original work, some translations, and some manifestos by young folks. We did this until 2012. But beginning in 2010, during the second government of Ahmadinejad, everything started to be disrupted: our books weren't coming out and our websites were getting shut down. Then in 2013, a center-right government came to power through the reformist wing of the Green Movement coalition's support and was very focused on using culture as a way of giving more social freedoms, rather than wider political or economic freedoms or gender equality. The privatization of cultural industries also intensified during Rouhani's government. So then our books started to come out again, which included original work, translations, and manifestos. But I was already outside of the country.

Claire Fontaine (CF) Introducing oneself is a very selective exercise, because one can tell several biographies of oneself: the academic one, the genealogical one, the political one. Of course, it's warmer to hear about the singular stories of people, where they were born and raised, whether one can identify with them or not. Then, there is a biographical narrative that offers the reader the emotional and social tools to classify someone in order to interact with them or their work constructively. This seems an innocent human activity but in fact it opens the doors to systematic misunderstandings and violent simplifications. We have created Claire Fontaine specifically to disarticulate the relationship between authorship and identity. We didn't like the idea of the artist as a brand for a recognizable body of work or writings; we also disliked the idea of authorship as a mirroring of one's own personality, as a form of property that expands the domain of what we are and just enlarges the enclosure of our professional reputation. We also often say that the existence of Claire Fontaine is the result of political impotence: the impossibility of experiencing life according to our political beliefs led us to create a space where we could exist and express affects and emotions that are repressed elsewhere. It wasn't a nostalgic attempt, but rather the will to save a political sensorium from its total extinction, with its specificity and its liberating powers. Claire Fontaine makes art but she also writes texts. She is a female artist composed of one person identifying as male and another person identifying as female, although being a man and being a woman are concepts that have been redefined since 2005 when Claire Fontaine had her first exhibition. However, if we were to introduce each of them it would be too long.

JR Thanks for those introductions! I want to start by talking about how the idea of the strike has evolved in recent years. This is something that stands out from the various waves of protest that have characterized the most recent cycle of struggles; struggles wherein the strike-tactic has been reconceived and has assumed a variety of names. There's the transnational social strike, the international women's strike, feminist strikes, rent strikes, debt strikes, and more recently Strike MoMA's call to "strike against modernity" and Louie Moreno's suggestive proposition to "wildcat the totality."[9] What defines the "human strike" as opposed to other forms is precisely its disidentification with the social function and subject position we occupy. The destituent/communist potential of the human strike defines it as a form of struggle that breaks with the form-determinations of capital and whose practical articulation can be defined in terms of "thinking against ourselves," as Claire Fontaine puts it:

> Thinking against ourselves will mean thinking against our identity and our effort to preserve it, it will mean stopping believing in the necessity of identifying ourselves with the place we occupy . . . . What we are looking at, then, is a movement of desubjectivisation and resubjectivisation, of exit from a condition . . . and an entrance into a new state, less defined, more uncertain, but freed of the weights that burdened the previous identity and allowed the perpetuation of the status quo.[10]

Perhaps we could say that, rather than being defined by its location within the processes of production or circulation, the human strike is first and foremost a reproductive struggle. It is a struggle over the reproduction of collective living and it expands the range of possible forms of everyday life *without reproducing value as the overdetermining form of social existence*. So, what does it mean to strike against capital today?

What are the types of activities that today define the strike and endow it with the potency to construct a noncapitalist or anticapitalist sociability? And what is the most helpful way of understanding the relation between various forms of struggles and how they relate to the conditions of the present, not simply in terms of their organizational forms but in terms of concrete modes of self-activity that constitute their material content?

CF We will begin—but we are also very interested in how Iman will respond, since questions like this are very delicate in places like Iran, where there is absolutely no freedom, where there is not even the commercial appearance of liberal freedom and human relations are openly colonized by control. We are currently working on the concept of the "refusal to work," which emerged from the Italian Autonomous movement of the 1970s. Refusing to work doesn't only mean abstaining from production, going on strike, or performing sabotage. When we work, we are always working on our professional identity, so what is fundamental to the refusal to work is the refusal to identify with the subjectivity of the worker. The refusal to work stems from the understanding that one's professional position alone can't be seen as the main participation in the community. And through the concept of class composition, the Autonomous movement drew attention to what was called the "excess of social needs," opposing the richness of the relationality between people outside of the party system and the workplace, to the grey anonymity of the perspective of political equality and the logic of equivalence between work, time, salary, and so on. There was a conscious sensuality and a new form of materialism emerging in this nonprofessional and nontraditionally political investment of life. An idea that the time shared outside of productive structures was more immediately subversive and richer than any organized struggle.

I would say that today this analysis is completely outdated. What is obvious from the vantage point of our present is that our current conditions of labor are characterized by the fact that the entirety of our subjectivity is constantly put to work, making it extremely difficult to differentiate between what is work and what is not. What we have just described is not a new condition in itself, since it already existed within informal economies in which people work and their clients are their friends: their life is completely intertwined with their survival. This is a condition that historically belongs to women and one that women have always understood and discussed: women never have a chance to rest, they can never shake off their responsibility, they never have fun (if they do it's dangerous), they never have the possibility of stopping their work because this might entail denying necessary help to a dependent creature. In this sense what is interesting about the idea of human strike is that it relates to Carla Lonzi's notion of the unplanned sensibility of the "unplanned subject."[11] For Lonzi the unplanned sensibility refers to the creation of something that exceeds mainstream representations and clichés and thus it is in excess to what is expected—i.e., the determinate social relations of a given patriarchal and heteronormative society. This sensibility invents the possibility for revolt and radical change where there seems to be no margin for transformation. The truth is that there is always an excess in human expression, even within the most constraining and mind-numbing use of social media. Even on Facebook interesting things can be found, and even on Zoom we can do amazing stuff, like this call. One must use polluted and potentially toxic tools to build spaces for freedom where life becomes different and relationships can be transformed. This is what interests us: the possibility of reproducing what we call the "hope-force," the "love-force," everywhere that there is room for the unexpected and the subversion of what oppresses us.

On the other hand, the sensibility that has created the refusal to work, and that can create the human strike, is a sensibility that has to do with what we call "magic materialism,"[12] a means to understand the materiality of what is alive and vitalizing as opposed to what is deadly. It's a way of reading causes and effects in energetic terms and not only by focusing on the material profit or the amount of products generated. Reproduction, care, exploitation, suffering, vitality, and illness must enter the equation that allows us to assess a situation, a productive or a political process. These are the stakes that have been continuously reasserted by Indigenous, feminist, and anti-racist movements, for which being unaccounted for was the starting point of their struggles. The presence of their bodies in public space, where they weren't expected to be, have at times already been forms of human strike.

To the question of what the human strike can do and what it cannot do or succeed at, we can say that "human strike" is just a name for a social phenomenon strongly related to what Fred Moten and Stefano Harney define with the term "study."[13] For instance, human strike is the *disarticulation* of the mechanisms that make everything functional and make everyone complicit in the processes that continue to destroy what is alive and healthy. It is a defunctionalization of struggle itself as a tool for reform, it's the immanence of self-transformation through the refusal of oppressive dynamics. So, it can happen in the workplace. It can happen in the family. It can happen anywhere. Any domain of social existence can host acts of human strike, and the important thing is to federate them.

This kind of act is a movement of the subject, molar and molecular. The many analyses of the pervasiveness of the society of control have shown that subjectivity is the privileged ground for the political transformation of society. In the current organization of the world, the grip of power has only tightened since the movements of the 1970s, which were truly defeated by the secret services, aka capillary and personal surveillance and the suspension of human rights through the state of exception, which today are systematic practices of government on a global scale. So, it has been understood that it's not enough to enforce governability by arresting people and threatening them with sanctions and violence. Their brains and their self-respect must be killed to convince them that uprising isn't worth it, because at the point that *nothing* is worth it, they might as well take part in a dying society in a dying world. That's why depression is such a pandemic. Human strike is a revolution in values, a revolution in the understanding of the value of oneself, an objection against "the conventional representation of life," as Jose put it. But we would really like to hear Iman speak on these issues.

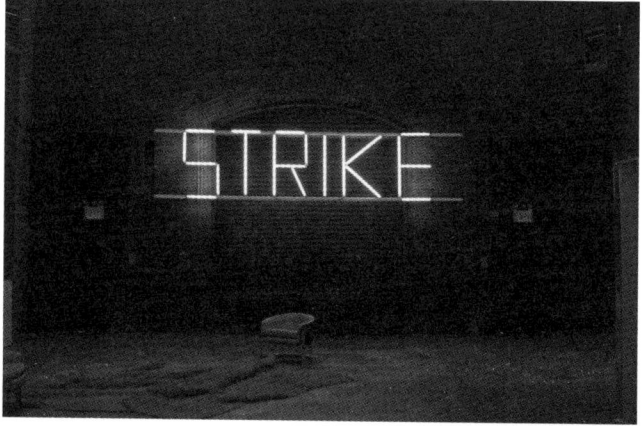

Claire Fontaine, *STRIKE (K. font V.I)*, 2005 (K. font). Wall mounted, white florescent tubes, red gelatine filters, transformers, spacers, movement detector and circuit-breaker. Courtesy Claire Fontaine.

IG I agree that at the end of the day, the nature of exploitation under the capitalist mode of production is global. If we were to put it in Marxian terms, we are dealing with the exacerbated effects of real subsumption. Of course, there are serious differences between the formal subsumption of economies in the Global North versus the Global South, and particularly in places like Iran, which as you mentioned is a very repressive country. But on the other hand, after more than a decade of liberal and neoliberal economic planning, the Iranian regime, and by extension Iranian society, have started to tolerate a certain "underground," for example, what can be found in the mainstream Western media about the sexual revolution in Iran.[14] Perhaps it will surprise many Western readers and comrades, but there is a very vibrant underground in Iran. Segments of younger generations have gone through processes of sexual (self-)liberation specific to the reality of being young and queer in Iran today. With the neoliberalization of the economy during the last three decades, the Islamic Republic understood that they needed a kind of underground that actively does not participate in mainstream society or makes its presence felt throughout society or public life, for the purposes of the reproduction of the political and economic organization of power specific to the country. So, the regime doesn't really interfere with this segment of the population. That said, if the underground begins to gain visibility, they will attack it viciously, as we saw in the 2010s.

And I mean all of this quite literally. The Iranian economy is an extractive economy whose foundations are built on oil production. As of a few years ago, it is an economy where more than 90 percent of workers are employed on temporary contracts. The effect of this parasitic relation on the lives of workers is seen via the proliferation of more indirect and intermittent access to both the market and the state. Thus, while capital continues extracting value from this intermittent coordination of collective labor, the labor of both precarious and nonprecarious workers, there continuously remains an excess or surplus that is not totally absorbed and that capital cannot appropriate. From what I understand by the term "human strike," I would say that it is via the collective cooperation within surplus populations that something like a human strike becomes possible.

With respect to what Jose said regarding the *other* forms the strike can assume today: there is a type of hyper-fragmentation of the reproductive and productive forces underway in Iran, as there is all over the world to differing degrees.

It is this process that makes salami out of social flesh, that transforms a collective body into a unity of segmented relations (e.g., through race, gender, sexuality, class, ethnicity, religion). On the other hand, there is a multiplication of different juridical forms of capture via different kinds of labor contracts that allow for the wage relation to coincide with the logic and demands of the market—flexibility, innovation, etcetera. What follows, of course, is the precaritization of labor that exacerbates this fragmentation. This twofold logic of segmentary relations and an ever more flexible labor market forms the recent context in Iran, and serves as the terrain of struggle for strike actions, such as the recent strikes of contracted workers, or what are also known as "project workers." These are workers who represent the most precarious elements of the national labor force and are hired on either temporary or zero-hour contracts for a duration of a particular project.

Now, what was interesting about the idea of human strike and its reception in Iran—both for myself and the comrades with whom I translated some of Claire Fontaine's essays—was the fact that the Iranian state did not view Claire Fontaine's writing as advancing a straightforwardly political program, and therefore did not censor our translations. By this I mean that any semblance of a program to seize the state via the formation of a new party is completely absent from the texts, which would be precisely the criteria used by the state to identify threats of subversion/opposition.

JR That makes sense, especially given the composition and organization of the recent strikes in Iran or even India, where workers mobilized outside points of production and assumed the tactic of the blockade typical of circulation struggles. It's in this context that the language and practice of the strike is being redefined for our present. This is a modality of struggle that is without any preexisting models to faithfully reproduce, such as a party program. I mean, it's not for nothing that the language of the strike was taken up in Argentina and Latin America in the wake of Argentina's destituent insurrection of 2001.[15] As recounted by Verónica Gago and Marta Malo, the language of the strike reinvigorated popular assemblies and opened lines of communication between individuals who would not have otherwise met, or anticipated standing alongside one another against the cops at a protest.[16] Given this posthumous birth of a strike do you find traces of the practices of Argentine comrades and militants, for instance, throughout the mobilizations in Iran?

IG Ah, yes. But only insofar as these practices are always translated, in both language and in application. In 2017, a thirty-two-year-old mother stood on an electrical box and waved her headscarf as if it were a flag. The next day, there was a nationwide protest by unemployed workers against the regime's proposed adjustments to the price of commodities. This simple act of that mother was then repeated by many women across the country and coincided with nationwide protest from various segments of the population over the increase in the price of food and the decrease in the purchasing power of their wages. The culmination of this activity was not only a renewal of the politics of everyday life in Iran, since the uprising that followed was severely suppressed. However, alongside the severity of state repression, and the regime's execution of an estimated 130 to 140 people with live ammunition in late 2017 and early 2018, you began to see a kind of secret solidarity, a kind of alliance that remained a public secret, between these different segmented forces of production. There were students, unemployed pensioners, women, queer activists—all of them went into the street with the unemployed.

Given that they were from such different segments of the population, in many cases this was the first time that some people heard certain accents. For those of Persian ethnicity, for example, some of the widely used slogans and chants were almost indecipherable. There were calls to form an alliance between these segmented groups, whose languages the Iranian left diaspora had to learn. Perhaps the most notable aspect of the uprising is that the initial mobilizations actually took place in marginal and peripheral cities, and only later appeared in Tehran. This political sequence demonstrates that the conditions were in place for a kind of strike that becomes a generalized mode of collectivity inherent to, or harbored within, these marginalized groups and surplus populations. The collectivity was the basis for these uprisings wherein dominant subjectivities were temporarily dissolved to make way for the construction of new modes of being. The problem, however, is that unlike the movements born out of the Arab Spring, where protestors stayed for one or two months at a given occupation and moved between different camps, experimenting with forms of living differently, the political context specific to Iran does not afford people a similar degree of creative mobility. To give but one example of the barbarism of such restrictive measures, during the protests in 2019, the state killed 1,500 people over the course of five days.

And yet, it is not always possible to recuperate the potential realized in the duration of struggles, or to renew that genetic structure that gives rise to new subjectivities or new forms of life, or to create an imagination of how to be together, or even to just broker new agreements once the insurrection has reached a certain apex in intensity. That said, I find it entirely appropriate to speak of the human strike in this context due to its differential and temporal structure. Thus, one of the human strike's modalities is the strike as a kind of insurrection, something that wants to put a stop to some processes. Sometimes a human strike is a kind of resistance that aims to slow down some processes. And other times, it's a labor of love, a being-together, which allows for groups to imagine different modes of collectivity. Since the social surplus is never entirely incorporated into the production process, the human strike can be found in different contexts—even in Iran, where the human strike unfolds under particular conditions and thus assumes a different appearance from those in the Global North.

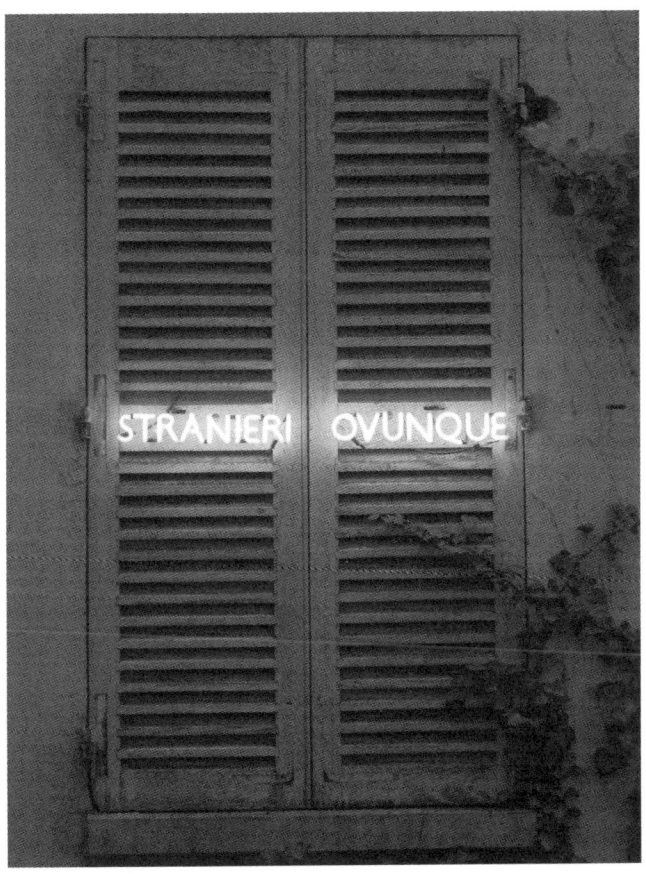

Claire Fontaine, *FOREIGNERS EVERYWHERE (STRANIERƎ OVUNQUE)*, 2024. Suspended, wall or window mounted cobalt blue neon, framework, electronic transformer and cables. Courtesy of Claire Fontaine.

To compare money with language is not less erroneous. Language does not transform ideas, so that the peculiarity of ideas is dissolved and their social character runs alongside them as a separate entity, like prices alongside commodities. Ideas do not exist separately from language. Ideas which have first to be translated out of their mother tongue into a foreign language in order to circulate, in order to become exchangeable, offer a somewhat better analogy: but the analogy then lies not in language, but in the foreignness of language.

—Karl Marx, *Grundrisse*

JR The reason that I thought of you both for this conversation was twofold: first, the shared commitment to thinking through the stakes and potentialities of the practice of theory that is no longer separated from the practice of living, and second, to further think through the human strike as it appears throughout the Global South. In fact, Iman and I continuously come back to Claire Fontaine's artwork, *Foreigners Everywhere*, while exchanging stories of our experiences living in different parts of Europe—and especially in places where we might be the only people of color and thus the places where one encounters the colonial gaze in its most naked state. Our joke is that this is what it must feel like to be Kafka's mysterious character Odradek, to be seen as an animate object without purpose, who is all the more unsettling due to the perceived absence of its reason for existing.[17] What does it mean to be a foreigner everywhere? A formulation like this evokes not only the so-called refugee crisis, but also the longstanding dynamics of estrangement, alienation, and generalized fragmentation characteristic of the organization of daily life via capitalist social relations. For someone like Benjamin, it's when we side with the working class that we ourselves become foreigners in our own country. In that sense, the foreignness in question plays on the fact that proletarians have no country and are themselves foreigners everywhere. Could we say that "foreignness" is an essential attribute or characteristic of the potential-as-content that inheres in every human strike? And how are we to understand and realize the latent power of foreignness against the foreigner that we have become with respect to ourselves, others, and the world?

In a previous interview Claire mentioned that the title "foreigners everywhere" is a reference to the name of an anti-racist, anarchist collective in Turin.[18] I was wondering if you could say a little more about that, especially with regards to the collective's more overt political engagements with you and your work.

CF A long time ago, we encountered a leaflet of a group that was called Stranieri Ovunque [Foreigners Everywhere], which was written in a similar style as Tiqqun. Even the layout and the image that was used were taken from Tiqqun, which of course had been taken from somewhere else—the chain of appropriation is infinite. But this group and their pamphlet had a very nice way of approaching the question of existential homelessness,[19] a generalized feeling that appeared before WWI, when the cosmopolitan dream of feeling everywhere at home began to fade. In the West the period of the two World Wars reflected back an image of a subjectivity that was nowhere at home in an industrially altered, violent, and colonized world; abstract art began to appear: representing the human figure had become increasingly problematic.

Foreigners Everywhere was inspired by this encounter and is a series of neon signs that deal with the violence of translation or the complexity of writing down oral languages. We illuminate these two words together in different idioms creating the ambiguity of a commentary on the location where the work is installed, it means as much that there are foreigners everywhere and that we are foreigners everywhere we go. This has probably been the most controversial work of ours. It has caused a lot of brutal reactions, and in some contexts even violence. One of our works was vandalized twice at the

10th Istanbul Biennial. It was not part of the *Foreigners Everywhere* series, but it revolved around the same idea. It was a large poster displaying a white space looking like a missing image and a text looking like its caption in Turkish and English. The idea was to reproduce the layout of Kafka's *Zürau Aphorisms*. The text was a quote from Benjamin that you referenced above, Jose: "whoever fights for the cause of the exploited is a foreigner in his own country." At first someone ripped the poster off the window, then the following day, because the poster was pasted from the inside to prevent them from ripping it off the glass, they shattered the window altogether. It was an offsite project that took place in a souk, so the work wasn't reinstalled for fear of more damage.

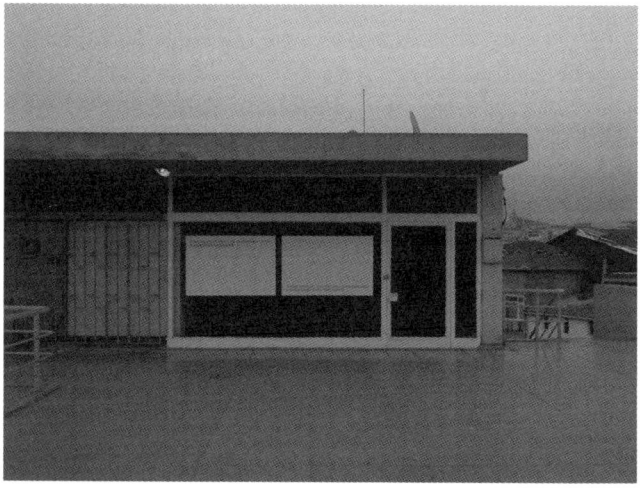

Claire Fontaine, *Affiches sans images*, (*Commentaires aux poèmes de Brecht, 1939*), 2007. Two pasted black and white photocopies. Courtesy of Claire Fontaine.

But to return to Iman's points about marginalization and the loss of productive power in Iran: it is interesting in relation to the contexts that created the ideas of refusal to work and class composition in Italy. For Autonomia in the 1960s and 1970s, the position of social marginality, of being outside of mainstream society, began to look like a resource to generate the communist potential of the autonomous movements. It was something that created a heterogeneous but vital social fabric where a different life and the energy for struggles were generated, because the margins were actually wonderful places to inhabit during that period. So, within the area of Autonomia, there was an idea of marginalization that has today become an aesthetic, but it is no longer an ethics. If we consider the way in which the theoretical appropriation of the '60s and '70s is carried out today, what is striking is that the expression of the marginality of that period—like *Radio Alice*, the fanzines, the posters, the fashion, the experimental movies—retain a specific power of attraction. Dozens of years later, mainstream culture is still seduced by these images of the past. So there was something going on there! Probably it was this claim of exteriority in relation to the squalor of society. This exteriority, this foreignness, is clearly something increasingly difficult to experience, because every domain of the desirable has been colonized by commodity. Commercial colonization has gone beyond the infrastructure and it has now reached the *infrathin*, which is, as Marcel Duchamp describes, a very subtle, almost imperceptible detail, a metaphysical quality that allows some objects to become readymades when others are nothing but banal tools for use. The infrathin is the warmth of a chair where someone was sitting before us, the point where the smoke of a cigarette coming out of the nostrils joins the one coming out of the mouth. It's a very subtle difference whose perception is only possible for people with an acute sensibility (in other words, people who aren't very busy). The relationship that we have to ourselves is mostly mediated by self-objectification: social, sexual, and professional life only know that single criterion for classifying the performances of the competitors. Contemporary sensorial disability is organized through social media, advertising, and commercial aesthetics, which always train and stimulate the reflexes useful for the consumer, to the detriment of the ones for the relationally creative being.

People have become less capable of being together, sharing space and time, not only because of repression and the closure of "alternative social spaces," but because of the way they invest the means of representation and self-representation at their disposal. Building the commons means building ourselves as the creatures that will thrive in it and help others do the same. That kind of capacity will not be encouraged by any kind of education available, nor the commercial or the pedagogical.

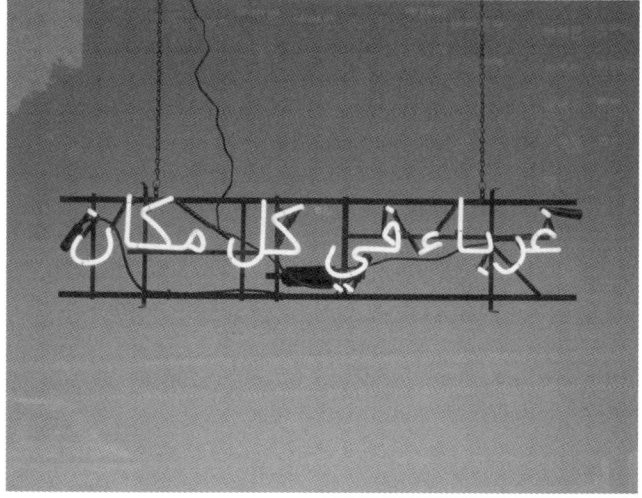

Claire Fontaine, *Foreigners Everywhere (Arabic)*, 2005 (Foreigners Everywhere). Suspended, wall or window mounted neon, framework, electronic transformer and cables. Courtesy Claire Fontaine.

JR Did you get a sense that the destruction of your work was undertaken by right-wing or neo-fascist groups, or that it was at least an expression of certain conservative tendencies with respect to the figure of the "foreigner"? It's already an open secret that Turkey has been holding the EU hostage at the bargaining table by threatening to allow migrants to pass through Turkey and into Western Europe.

CF Well, with our first show in New York City at Reena Spaulings, we showed a neon sign that read "Foreigners Everywhere" in Arabic in the window, and there were many complaints from the neighborhood.

JR In Soho?

CF Yeah, it was the first place they had their space. They ultimately lost their lease due to the number of complaints from the neighborhood. I mean, Kate Hardy projected a porn movie on the facade of the building, but it didn't bother people as much.

There were also problems when we exhibited the same work in Serbia. This is to say: we are currently living through the exacerbation and deepening of the feeling of being threatened by the other, especially in light of the pandemic, which has done nothing but feed fascism. To be socially distant from others one needs to be emotionally distant from them. Without missing a beat, fascism then feeds back into the culture of fear while also assuming countless forms. So we are continuously becoming ever more ignorant of our collective potentiality.

IG Both of your comments confirm my feeling that this idea of being a foreigner everywhere—being a traitor to your own class, race, gender—remains connected to what has been happening in Europe since 2014–2015: the resurgence of ultra-right-wing movements and the mobilization of fear. Fear is being mobilized by and for the privileged, who are fearful of losing said privileges, the loss of which is equated with the loss of freedom itself. Thinking from my own experience, experiences shared with Jose and other friends, I have the sense that the most visible expression of demonized alterity is within the legal field. When you think about it, it is foreigners who are always admitted entry on freelance visas or student visas, visas that are temporary and therefore determine their mode of existence as always being on the threshold of legal/juridical subjectivity.

JR Because to be a foreigner is to not have any rights. So, for instance, if one doesn't have access to healthcare or a wage, then that usually means you can only sell the use-value you have left, which is your body, and get by with the only forms of relief at your disposal. I mean, foreigners don't go to Germany because it is "exotic," because of its acceptance of that which Islam or non-Western societies prohibit. If foreigners are demonized for engaging in sex work and drug use, as they have been by German media outlets, they are demonized for resolving the question of how to continue to reproduce themselves, on their own terms, and within an asylum process that does not care whether their needs are met or not.

IG Exactly. And this legal threshold that defines their entire mode of being reveals the way in which foreigners are neither inside nor outside the reach of statist recognition and capture. Of course, this means that the state encourages foreigners to maintain their livelihood within this threshold until the moment they are granted full recognition by the state. In the meantime, one wrong move and you are immediately designated as illegal. And even after being granted full recognition you are once again subjected to the metropole's spatial logic of division insofar as communities are reproduced as segregated identity-groups, as is the case with many cities across Europe that I have visited—all the Iranians are together, all the Kurds are together, and so on. Moreover, there is the persistent struggle over whose subject-position places them closer to the privileges of the system. So, being on the threshold of legality makes it very hard for these people to withhold their labor, to withhold their participation in the integration process, or even to refuse to learn the German language. In most cases, if the foreigner wants to reject one's complicity with the mockery of civility that is state power, or to reject statist capture as an asylum seeker, the foreigner still finds themselves "obliged" (i.e., threatened with police violence and deportation) to successfully convince the state that they are incapable of every possible form of employment made available to them.

At the same time, when the refugee movement happened in Berlin in 2012—whose symbolic sites were the asylum seekers' occupation of Oranienplatz and the Gerhart Hauptmann high school near Görlitzer Park—it was a show of solidarity by the German left with the most precarious people in Germany.[20] When the refugees marched from their camp, the police enforced the state's policy of *Residenzpflicht*: Germany's policy of mandatory residency within an arbitrarily delimited boundary issued to asylum seekers by the local immigration office [*Ausländerbehörde*]. In fact, upon arriving in Germany, refugees are required, by law, to remain in their assigned camps from anywhere between six weeks to six *months*. And of course, they don't have the right to work, or the right to access any other form of social welfare, except a state-sanctioned monthly allowance of no more than four hundred euros. These are some of the reasons that led them to march to Berlin and occupy Oranienplatz and the nearby school. Upon arrival, they were met with the solidarity of an international network of activists and a variety of leftist groups from the post-New Left generation. And it was very interesting to see this recomposition of various segments of the German left, such that adherents of older currents of German Marxism seemed to realize relations of solidarity and the warmth of camaraderie with people who were mostly from West Asia and North Africa. In this kind of situation where there are "foreigners everywhere," so to speak, we also discover the potentiality for realizing a human strike.

CF I feel that Carla Lonzi's notion of illegibility aligns with what both of you are saying, since she describes her own revolt and politicization in a similar way. For example, in her diaries, she writes about hanging out at a dinner with some people who are nice but could never grasp her or understand the world as she sees it. She comments, "I don't want to make a drama about this because it is a drama." For us, this notion of illegibility is at the core of the human strike because when these illegible lives federate with one another, it is no longer possible to continue this game of oppressive identity that proceeds by projecting otherness onto anyone one wants to discriminate. And in its place, these illegibilities show how they were always overwritten, always unseen, always belittled in the name of their supposedly essential foreignness or marginality. Seeing this phenomenon as something that can be undone is very refreshing. Similarly, slogans from '77 in Italy that defunctionalize even the political claim as a meaningful form of struggle—"more churches, less houses," "politicians are innocent, we are the real delinquents," and so on—are a way of immediately exiting emotional, intellectual, and material poverty, refusing the position of victim, to show instead the desire for joy, the capacity for irony, the distrust towards a depressing and inacceptable reality. It's a claim to get the right to flourish and love each other at the very moment when the state says: you should just be alone and miserable.

In the case of refugees, however, this arbitrary use of power by nation states gives rise to ever more terrifying forms of immiseration. It would be unsettling for governments if the Western population suddenly empathized with the people dying in the Mediterranean or rotting in the camps, if they saw them as their children, their friends, people that could be their neighbor or their colleague. It's an impossible thought, that they are hungry, tortured, psychologically scarred, right now, whilst we are grocery shopping or making a phone call. Mass production of naked life, otherness, racialization of the other through the police and the media are an antidote to this possibility. So it seems that the political category of *illegibility* can help us develop the kind of political sophistication that we need in order to not lose our minds, in a context where belonging to a country, a culture, or a social class has become something so fragile for so many that it can't protect them from being dispossessed and yet it's harbored by the political right to create and exclude the Other. Illegibility is not a horizon, like opacity or clandestineness, but a political category to read the existing present. It is not simply an analytical idea but a therapeutic one since it responds to the very basic need to describe the situations of legal, existential, and political exclusion. I mean, why would someone who is a foreigner flee their country in order to endure new forms of exclusion and violence in exchange for material survival? Why does hospitality need to become the humiliation of the guest?

Now, one of the ways you can twist this situation involves doing something that doesn't cohere with normative images and standardized representations of the excluded—like what Elia Suleiman, Kamal Aljafari (who is a friend of ours), and other Palestinian artists and filmmakers do, when they make artworks that refuse to just document the horror of their situation as a people. Instead, they do things that are unexpected. They claim the space of ease, of joy, of freedom for themselves, they refuse a moral duty that will imprison them and their cause. Because if one accepts the position of misery, the best things that one can hope for are the pity of the people who are not in the same situation, their compassion, their guilt, their condescension. This just paves the way for more separation and dishonesty, it opens the route for spectators to slide into neutrality and distance. Disarticulating the binary division between oppressed and oppressors is a vital necessity. Partly because the position of the oppressed is more insightful and richer than the one of the oppressor, but it so in ways that defy the aesthetics and the ethics of the latter, revealing why violence is impoverishing for the ones who practice it as much as for the ones that endure it. The oppressor can be passive, can be disinterested in the case of the ones he is contributing to damage, he can be totally unaware of his position, because it is legalized and normalized by the system. Neutrality, indifference, and emotional deafness are of course variations of this violence, and this is the problem of the ones who *aren't* refugees, who *aren't* really foreigners anywhere. As the Italian feminists used to put it: the world needs women's freedom. Women's liberation is not women's problem, it's the world's problem, because without it the planet is nothing but a poor and cruel place. It's obvious why the freedom of oppressed people would make society a much more interesting and a more intelligent social space for everyone. It's not a moral consideration, but a practical one. Ceasing to oppress is better than ceasing to be oppressed.

IG About two months ago, I was writing a critique of human rights discourse with respect to the massacre that happened in Iran in 1988. At the same time, I was reading a text of yours, Claire Fontaine. And what was interesting for me about human strike in comparison to the idea of human rights was the act of reclaiming a conception of the human. And one of the problems in Germany, for example, is precisely this discourse which claims that refugees are welcome, that Germany is hospitable, and so on. Problems arise because the country positions itself as the host rather than the guest—the guest whose freedom of residence is entirely dependent on the good will of its host country. Hence you have people from Angela Merkel to the German public who genuinely believe in this discourse of German hospitality and simultaneously see no problem with the state's process of regulating the flow of bodies, which begins with relocating refugees into camps, then into job centers that only afford them the most precarious jobs in the formal economy. And the problem here is that the *other* of state recognition is rendered intelligible insofar it is stripped of its heterogeneity.

I saw an example of this when I went to the Foreigner's Office in Berlin. Inside there was a poster of a young woman whose image projected European values of beauty: first of all, she was white, but she also had piercings. And sure, she was very beautiful. However, underneath her image a message read: "I am a refugee. I have a dream." But if you go to the Ausländerbehörde and look at all the refugees who are there, none of them are white! I come back to the question of what it means to be a foreigner in a country. When I fled from Iran and reflected upon its state of affairs from the distance of exile, it was clear that our practices were informed by this notion of being a foreigner in one's own country. But when you look at the lives of marginalized populations, they are really foreigners in their own country. In Iran, for example, there are thousands of Baluchi people in the south that don't even have national identity cards.

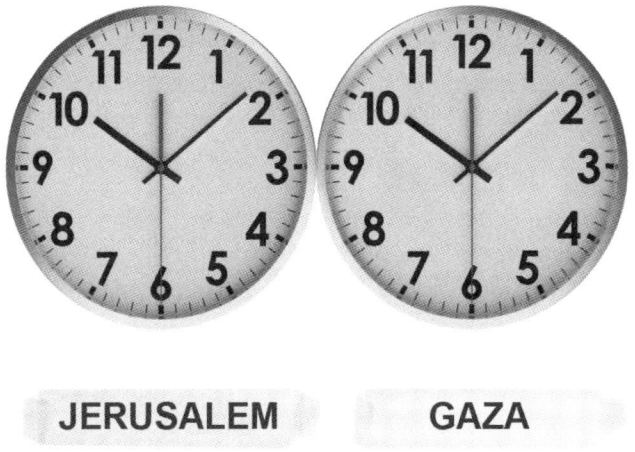

JERUSALEM   GAZA

Claire Fontaine, *Untitled (same war time zone)*, 2016–18. Mains/battery operated wall clock, printed paper and masking tape. Courtesy of Claire Fontaine.

CF Germany's state hospitality is stained by colonialism because Germany is a Zionist country. Its way of overcoming the consequences of its own shameful and disgusting nationalism has been to support somebody else's shameful and disgusting ethno-nationalism, to wash out its guilt. Ultimately this kind of charity is a form of utter contempt, a tool of political rehabilitation. The fact that the European Union is so informed and inspired by Germany says everything about how it wishes to forget and forgive the past. Presenting Germany as a model of tolerance, hospitality, and integration is mind-blowing, really mind-blowing. The wounds of colonialism and fascism are still open and infected: France only recently admitted to the systematic torture of Algerians during the war. The political position of France and its selective hospitality are also very interesting in this respect. Recently France and Italy agreed to send back Italian refugees from the Mitterand times to serve a prison sentence pronounced in another century. In this respect, *Homo Sacer* by Agamben remains a very, very relevant philosophical work and probably the core of all his philosophical oeuvre alongside *Remnants of Auschwitz* and *The Time That Remains*, because it tackles the way in which democracies are as much based on human rights as they are on their suspension: the state of exception. How police and the industrial production of naked life are the backbone of capitalism. In Agamben's work, unfortunately, there isn't even a shade of a feminist perspective, but the book that we always quote by the Milan Women's Bookstore, in Italian titled *Don't Believe You Have Any Rights*, shows us how we can anyway think outside the model of subsumption, integration, inclusion through feminism.[21] As Moten and Harney put it, we have the right to refuse rights, we have the right to refuse what has been refused to us. We don't have to believe humiliating lies. Today we can see how inclusion is based on the self-hatred of the included and the denial of their personal and collective past.

JR I just want to comment on Iman's example of the occupation at Oranienplatz, since there are a couple of things worth noting here. For one, the cardinal practical and theoretical virtue of this younger generation of European leftists was the way that Berlin's decentralized network of house projects and autonomous spaces was able to immediately organize individual rooms for most, if not all, of the refugees that participated in the occupation at Oranienplatz. This was the case especially when there was no longer a question of "if they will be arrested" but a question of "when they will be arrested." What does it mean to be evicted via the state-sponsored violence of the police? How can you evict those who are already without a home? And if it is impossible to evict those who are already homeless, then they will be made to undergo the impossible. In light of all this violence, Berlin's decentralized network of housing initiatives moved beyond symbolic gestures and realized material relations of solidarity in the form of housing, which remains, in my opinion, an achievement in its own right. It marks the expansion of what this autonomous network can collectively do just as it points out the lie of the authoritarian leftist fetish of "scalability." The seductive presumption of this scalability rejoinder is that autonomous forms of self-organization are fundamentally incapable of addressing crises of social reproduction that extend beyond the provincial localism of the "anarchist neighborhood" and the "temporary autonomous zone." It was precisely this fetish for scale that was shown to be the red herring that it most often is and refuted via the collective practice of autonomous self-organization.

But slowly, after this initial increase in the capacities of this autonomous network, divisions began to appear within some of the houses. The reason for this was that some of the refugees who were housed felt estranged despite this concrete and material gesture of solidarity. And friends (majority white) who helped organize this action didn't realize, until it was already too late or too difficult to address, that the refugees wouldn't really engage with them (their hosts), that there was no real bond other than the initial gesture, which now retained the bitter taste of charity. Once these issues were made common knowledge, the whole problem that conditioned this relation of solidarity revealed a fragmentation internal to each house project's organization of domestic life. The problem was not a question of organizational form (centralized versus decentralized) but how even the most militant comrade can reproduce the estrangement from which they helped you escape.

IG And as we know, Islam was one of these divisive issues in these spaces, since a majority of refugees were practicing Muslims. But if you go to a squat or house project in Berlin, there is alcohol, sexual liberty, and so on. So, there were different forms of life that at times could not coexist, just as there were instances of informal, and house-run, education programs where fights would break out over the question of Palestine—something that is not surprising since many of these house projects are aligned with *Antideutsche* to a greater or lesser extent.[22] But if you are from West Asia or North Africa, Palestinian liberation is obviously a popular issue. Given the circumstances, conflict was inevitable. What is more, for many of my POC friends and feminist or radical feminist friends in the anti-imperialist camp, they confronted the twofold problem of sexism and racism within these spaces.

JR Experiences and stories like these brought me back to the idea of the human strike as a strike against the subjects we have been made to become in exchange for the right to be exempted from the most brutal forms of state violence. The right to exemption from violence is like any right—it can be revoked at any time. And for me, these problems are intimately related to what I think Claire Fontaine so eloquently raised in her comparative analysis of Lonzi, Benjamin, and Brecht in "Raising the Uprising"—particularly the discussion of Benjamin's review of Brecht's *The Mother.* These are probably some of the most striking two to three pages in your most recent published text:

> Pelagea 'adopts' communism and Benjamin writes that 'she is loved by Communism as only a mother is loved: she is loved not for the sake of her beauty or her fame or her excellence, but as the inexhaustible source of help. She represents help at its source, where it is pure-flowing, where it is practical and not false, that can still be channeled without reservations toward what, without reservations, needs help—namely Communism. The mother is the praxis incarnated.'[23]

All of this is presented as a virtue and the basis of communist society. But here we again encounter the questions posed by the human strike. What would it mean to struggle alongside others in a way where the form of life that is produced does not rely on value or is not wholly defined by value? How can it produce a form of life that is not defined by more direct forms of domination (racialized and gendered violence) as a means of conflict resolution; a form of life no longer defined by the kind of ignorance that covers up what in France is called "*racisme quotidien*" and in the US gets called "micro-aggressions"? The problems that we still inherit from figures even as beloved as Benjamin and Marx are that these issues of social reproduction are overlooked or misunderstood—and they are problems that continue to lack a solution.

Seen in this way, communism no longer appears so certain of itself. That is to say, if Marx could still write, in 1844, that "Communism is the riddle of history solved" and that "knows itself to be" such, after '68 and especially after '77, communism is no longer so certain of itself. Thus, could we say that, today, it is *communism that appears as the riddle posed to history?*

CF Well, it's not really a riddle. There are many ways of seeing what communism could mean, some of which have become clearer today than in the past. At least over the past fifteen years, the idea of communism is no longer that of appropriating the means of production, because the means of production, along with what is being produced, are themselves destroying the planet. So this is already a revolution in the very foundations of the philosophical framework of materialism, which historical communism and the workers movement sought to realize as praxis. But this isn't a riddle, it was a mistake from the very beginning and remains the structuring blind spot of Marxism and workerist ideologies. For example, we were re-reading the political journal *Quaderni Rossi*, and Raniero Panzieri in particular, who conceives of political economy as a system of projection of values. But what becomes clear when returning to these texts are several errors that misled the dream of communism in Italy. During the '60s and '70s, and unlike its counterparts in neighboring European countries, Italy was singular for having a breed of communism that was inseparable from a complete rejection of Stalinism. This produced a very advanced theoretical elaboration and practice in the extra-parliamentary parts of the left, creating incredible movements that truly had revolutionary potential. With the "Historic Compromise"[24] and the Calogero theorem[25] we saw this entire process neutralized through a political genocide of the protagonists of '77 that ended up causing a progressive erosion of the very identity of the communist party. Italy no longer has a communist party, but this immense political absence isn't experienced as a loss. Because the party itself was an error, it constituted *one of these wrong representations of what communism could be.* It was a representation of communism incapable of making good on the promise of *Gemeinwesen* as a social and concretely shared reality.[26]

Communism is also an epistemic system that provides tools for the analysis of reality, a model of sociability and social relations that are beyond extraction, exploitation, alienation: this is communism understood as the possibility of having a discourse coherent with one's life. It's something that Foucault develops in his analysis of the production of subjectivities and the various forms of power that correspond to their respective forms of society (pastoral, disciplinary, biopower, and so on). Seen in this light, the program of communism is one of seizing the means of the production and reproduction of subjectivities that can also refuse to simply be useful or productive, to be a workforce at the service of a collective or private project. The collective must serve the singularities and not vice versa, otherwise who will reproduce the struggle-force and the love-force to keep collectives alive? If collectives don't provide strength for their members, they will just desert them and try to survive outside of them, in the familiar isolating system. There is work involved in reproducing oneself as a part of any social formation; within a communist society this work should be accounted for and rewarded, it should be part of the process of attribution of value to people, objects, time. And here we return to one of

the core questions of Autonomia and the workerist movement: the independence of salary from work. But capital has
already made this idea a reality that we are witnessing today.
The wealthiest individuals have jobs that are the most parasitic and damaging to the planet. So wealth has lost even the
slightest respectability on the political level. Now when we
are talking about what communism should and could be—
and I am hesitant to invoke Heidegger here but I must—have
we, in fact, not yet begun to *think* the potential promise of
communism? Thinking about it, the very categories we use
when theorizing do not allow us to grasp a coherent form
of life that corresponds to a future that is livable. This dogmatic image reduces communism to a form of collectivity,
grounded on what is shared rather than exchanged, but
whose end remains the vague hope of collectively opposing
the disasters of capitalism.

There's been so much confusion about what patriarchy
has done and how it informs all of these dreams of living
together, to the point that one wonders if humanity is nothing other than the thought of white (cis-)men. So we have
reached a time where we must think of a *communism without
patriarchy*, and to do so would lead to something completely
different. One reason is that this would transform the collective perception of resources and inform a specific sensibility
toward the energy of living beings and natural resources. It
would be a communism where the spontaneous and normalized extraction of the capacities of others to their detriment would be absent. This would be a transformation in
the very balance between production and reproduction and
would open the possibility of identifying the different forms
of work and care that make productivity and profit possible
for some, impossible for others. Because exploitation takes so
many forms and we haven't even started to recognize them
all, we only see the impoverishment without connecting it to
its multiple causes.

Our present will be defined by the possibility of thinking
and elaborating a communism that has learned from these

past mistakes. But this idea of what communism could be is also the solution to the evils of mass surveillance and counter-insurgency. It could provide a healthy social life. In its place they sell us self-organization as a new horizon of self-exploitation: Uber, Airbnb, Zoom, etc. These are not forms of cooperation for the common good. People settle for a society of zero solidarity and minimum unwanted social contact. It's quite insane because without redefining the forms of recognition of our mutual humanity beyond class, race, and gender differences, we can't even ensure the survival of the planet in the new future.

IG I couldn't agree more. We need to redeem the idea of communism, an idea that is itself constantly worked upon and renewed by criticism. That said, one of the most important problems with what communism became under "really existing socialism" was this idea of being responsible for History—a responsibility that is not only due to our complicity in the immiseration of others, but also due to the assumption that what makes political subjectivity revolutionary is that the subject acts *in the name of* both past and present. This framework is a by-product of the mistaken idea that the proletariat's authentic appropriation of History is equal to the real movement that abolishes itself and the present situation. And therefore, Marx is correct in saying that the British are responsible for the violence and bloodshed of their colonization of India, which arises from their position of the civilized steward of all that the colonized were said to be unfit to oversee: self-organization, self-governance, rational distribution and consumption of resources, and so on. This is also what Engels talks about when he calls upon the proletariat of Germany and France to support the British armies in their war against the Ottoman Empire, because the Turks were said to be barbarians. This way of utilizing the language of the "historical destiny" of the proletariat remains one of the major problems of historical communism. We should be clear, though, that Marx does understand that the condition of wage labor is slavery and the production of surplus populations. So he is not totally blind to anticolonial struggles insofar as his critique of political economy understands these struggles to be against value and the capitalist mode of production, which is predicated on processes of racialization and gender domination both at home and in public.

Many struggles have attempted and continue to struggle against communism bound to the party-form, which is what we saw in the feminist movements of the '70s and what continues today with the Kurdish liberation struggle, particularly in the late '90s and early 2000s, and after Turkey arrested Abdullah Öcalan (with the help of the US). Before this period, the Kurdistan Workers' Party (PKK) was very much a Marxist-Leninist organization and was not invested in developing consciousness around issues of gender, sexuality, or even race. But with the end of the '90s and Öcalan's arrest, we see an internal revolt throughout the organization *and* a women's revolt within the PKK. And the most visible consequence of this revolt against the party-form is the Rojava experiment, which has been incredibly liberatory for women in that region.

But this doesn't mean that the Kurdish struggle has arrived at a position that is untouched by the problems posed by the history of class struggle or the history of anticolonial struggle. To the contrary, the principle of development for Rojava has been a permanent internal criticism of themselves as well as their material conditions. So this problem of subjectivity that comes out of the '60s and '70s gains importance in this context. The discussion is no longer limited to the meaning of subjectivity afforded by capitalist social relations; it has become a conversation about the kinds of subjectivities that are possible via the abolition of both capital and the authoritarian political forms assumed during previous cycles of struggle—e.g., the party-form, the state, the union, and so on. It is no longer possible to imagine revolution as the collective usurpation of state power in order to guide the masses to paradise, which is what the Islamic Republic of Iran or Turkey are currently trying to do.

JR Fitting remarks on the nine-year anniversary of the Rojava experiment, Iman. And to the chagrin of the Islamic Republic but to our delight, there is more than one way to get to paradise.

IG [*Laughs.*] Indeed, *azizam!*

JR That said, maybe we should save our remarks on these and related topics for the next time we meet. For now, I just want to thank you both for this conversation.

IG Thank you, Jose. And thank you, Claire Fontaine. This was really great. When I was reading and translating your work in Tehran, I never thought that I would meet you.

CF I was going to say the same. Thank you, Iman and Jose. It's been wonderful speaking with both of you. I was worried that we would not be able to connect all our respective points of interest, but there was absolutely no problem. We speak the same language.

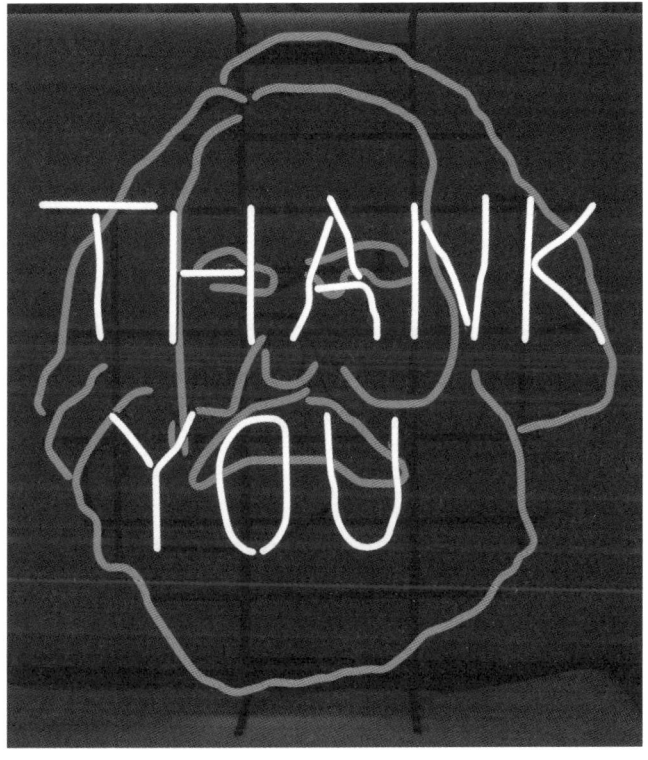

Claire Fontaine, *Untitled (Thank-you)*, 2004. Neon glass, electrodes, transformers, flasher unit and framework. Wall or window mounted. Courtesy of Claire Fontaine.

AFTERWORD

THE BITTER EXPERIENCE OF WORKERS IN IRAN: FROM THE GENERAL TO اعتصاب انسانی

Workers in Iran have been on general strike for the past thirteen days. Employed by contractor companies in the oil industry, the strike has reached more than seventy industrial hubs and more than sixty thousand workers are currently taking part. What is significant in this general strike is the orientation toward connecting the struggles of the most precarious workers who have either temporary or zero-hour contracts—so-called "project workers"—with the struggle of workers in possession of any degree of job security whatsoever. The hierarchy that is imposed on "project workers," which organizes their fragmentation as a group and renders every intra-class alliance impossible, is a horrifying and complex process. The history of general strikes led by workers at the National Iranian Oil Company (NIOC) is just as much a story of violence as it is a story of their destituent potential. We should not forget that, in 1979, Iranian oil workers helped bring about the downfall of the Pahlavi Monarchy.

The strikers work for companies contracted by the NIOC, which is in the process of economic (neo)liberalization that began in the early '90s. What resulted from this period was the trend of outsourcing work to different forms of private contractor companies and the consequent precaritization of labor.

A labyrinth made up of contractor companies are active in the Iranian oil industry, some of which work mainly with the NIOC. The larger companies also contract different jobs and services to other, smaller contractors. There are also human resource contractor companies that make contracts with workers and distribute them to other larger or smaller contractors. Inside contractor companies, different forms of contract exist: employed workers with fixed terms contracts; temporary workers with contracts under a year; temporary workers with monthly or daily or zero-hour contracts. There are even "oral" contracts between some of these workers and their contractor employers. Wages differ widely between these groups.

Prior to contract labor's predominance, an income gap was already present between the NIOC's white-collar employees and blue-collar workers. The conditions for this uptick in immiseration started with the hideously manipulative process of turning blue-collar workers into white-collar workers. The blue-collar workers could still agitate for (higher) wages and insurance under the national labor law and go on strike for their demands. But the white-collar employees were under NIOC terms of employment and did not have the right to refer to the national labor law and its regulations and already limited possibilities for workers' right to assemble and protest. Looking at the benefit gap between themselves and white-collar employees, many blue-collar workers accepted white-collar contracts. But of course, according to NIOC regulations about expertise and form of labor, they stayed with lower income and fewer benefits. Unable to complain according to the labor law, many were faced with two options: starvation wages or early retirement with a lump sum. Many selected the second option. After many workers were basically thrown out, the NIOC started outsourcing labor, and the intense precaritization of its labor force began.

Other lines of fragmentation exist within the labor market besides contracted and subcontracted labor, such as ethnicity/race and gender. Production within Iran's oil industry is largely concentrated in the country's southern region, where the composition of labor is largely Arab and Lor populations and other minorities. The local people are those who are employed with the lowest wages and have the most precarious contracts. Women are much less present in the oil industry in Iran, and few of them work as official white-collar employees. The rest work in services such as domestic labor and other forms of care work that are also characterized by very precarious conditions. It is evident that such hyper-categorization and fragmentation creates different "interests" among the oil industry workers. For instance, one of the main divisions is that which exists between unofficial workers (those who are working with contractor companies) and "official workers" (who are employed by the NIOC and are in strategic positions with regards to production). Such fragmentation of the workforce has demonstrable effects on and sets limitations on the workers' struggle. Many statements by different unions and precarious workers, the women's movement and feminists, pensioners, truck drivers, teachers, nurses, and so on have expressed their support for the strikers with displays of solidarity. This was visible during the 2021 May Day festivities, when various organizations called for protests or supported protests to improve living conditions. Workers were once the symbol of the lower class, but the coalition that has emerged in recent protests through the declaration of solidarity, including in the case of May Day, is more demographically diverse and therefore more pervasive. Government retirees, teachers, nurses, contract workers, drivers, women, the unemployed, apprentices, ranchers, farmers, industrial workers, and other small-scale producers are all now part of this protesting coalition, all making calls to end neoliberalization and precaritization of labor. When contract workers publicized their call for a general strike, the "precariat" of the Iranian oil industry, which is the main source of GDP in Iran, they included the demands of the "official" workers as well. If the demands of the contract workers were not met, the "official" workers were supposed to join the strike on June 30, 2021. In the end, they did not suspend their collective labor. However, some of them organized protest marches and showed solidarity with the project workers.

Truck drivers, another segment of the composition of the industry's precarious labor force, distributing goods such as oil, have also shown solidarity with oil project workers. Some of them have joined the strike. Some bus drivers staged a protest in support of oil workers and they have also voiced their own demands. The government is already trying to intensify the fragmenting lines between workers to slow down the protests and break the strike. By outsourcing work to contractor companies, NIOC has multiplied the number of bosses facing the workers and the ministry takes no responsibility for "unofficial" workers. But at the same time, the parliament passed regulations to increase the benefits for "official" workers. The contractor companies have already fired hundreds of these so-called "project workers" with zero-hour contracts in different centers.

Workers in Asaluyeh—the site for the facilities of the huge Pars Special Energy Economic Zone (PSEEZ) project— live in crowded camps set up by their employers, with poor hygiene measures while the average daily temperature is approximately 41 degrees Celsius (105.8 F). Meanwhile, their employers, in coordination with the security apparatus, have limited food and water deliveries or ended them altogether. If that wasn't enough, workers have been blocked from using their phones and the internet. To the workers, it is clear that their employers want them to leave the camp, thus ending their strike. Undeterred, workers opted to communize their resources and purchase water tankers themselves. The tradition of orthodox Marxism still dominant in the region has long been criticized for equating the factory with the site of communist organizing. This assumption assumes that the factory is the site that entails the greatest degree of

The Map of Workers Strike in Iran's Petroleum Industry
The Map of Workers Strikes in Iran's Petroleum Industry 2020 and 2021

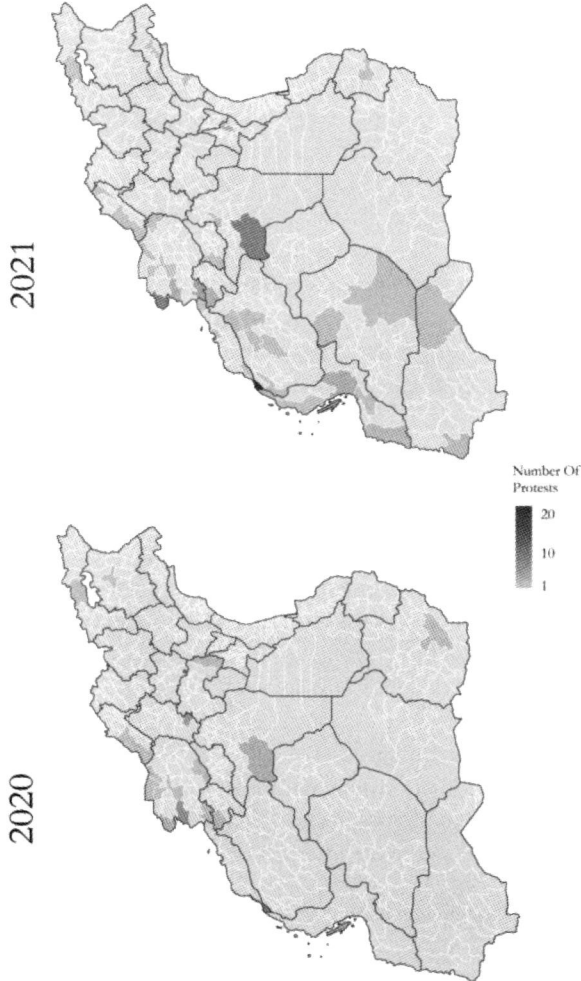

The raw data for these maps are news articles published in *Hrana*, *Akhbar-e Rooz*, and *Radio Zamaneh*. The 2020 map covers strikes reported from August 1 to September 6, 2020, and the 20201 map covers strikes from June 19 to August 2, 2021. Source: Middle East Research and Information Project, merip.org.

revolutionary potential given that it convenes workers in one space and around machinery that inevitably necessitates communication and cooperation. This cooperation has an excess that cannot be absorbed in the reproduction cycle, which led certain Marxist currents to posit the factory as capable of creating conditions for revolutionary organization of the workers. The precarious workers with different forms of temporary contracts with contractor companies are often working in the same space as those with fixed contracts, and/ or who are official employees of the Iranian Oil Company. But this has not fully surpassed the process of accumulation or the complementary process of the accumulation of misery. And it is via this relentless compulsion toward the organiza-tion of this body of collective labor that Capital continues to make salami out of social flesh. Looking at what is happening right now, there is an excess of cooperation, of a kind of labor of love (the language of equality and solidarity), that cannot be absorbed even through hyper-fragmentation of the labor force. A strike that begins not from waged labor but from the ever growing surplus population that is continuously (re-)produced by the accumulation of value under capital, is the material precondition for transforming struggles that have been historically reformist in essence (e.g., struggles over wages, labor conditions, pensions, etc.) into a gener-alized struggle against the forms of direct domination that define the production process and the extra-economic forms of indirect domination that reinforce, our reality as one of dependence on markets and states for mere subsistence. This type of strike is precisely what Claire Fontaine understands with the concept of the "human strike," a kind of strike not simply against the circuits of production but one that seeks to wildcat this totality wherein every form-of-life is but a form-of-value.

—Iman Ganji and Jose Rosales,
Amsterdam and Lisbon,
July 9, 2021

VOLUME 3

LOOTING

Saidiya Hartman, Christina Sharpe,
and Rinaldo Walcott,
moderated by Vicky Osterweil

The following conversation with Saidiya Hartman, Christina Sharpe, and Rinaldo Walcott was held in fall 2022, two years after the fires of the George Floyd rebellion had faded. It took place in a period of long reactionary retrenchment and ennui, driven by the exacerbation and denial of the COVID-19 pandemic and fascist attacks on reproductive health and queer life.[1] The forgetting of the uprising has been a crucial part of this reaction, and is an active and ongoing process. When it is remembered, it is referred to more in terms of its mass national scope and character than its attacks on property and police.

It is in the interests of white supremacy to claim that rioting and looting are not communicative acts, that they are rather pure "criminality," an unleashing of the monstrous id of that state of nature lurking behind the everyday. This is what fascists and the police endeavor to prove when they themselves riot, most infamously in recent memory in Charlottesville, wantonly killing and destroying in a frenzy of hatred. Framed this way, riots—especially those fighting against and in response to police violence—justify the "Thin

Blue Line" in all its obscenity and overreach: it's the pigs or the mob.

But the sustained rejection and erasure of antipolice and black-led rioting and looting—by the state, the academy, the media, corporations, as well as many leftist and social-ist groups—only indicates just how much ideological work it takes to repress the message of the riot.

The riot refuses to "speak truth to power"; it refuses to address capital and its nation states, and so politicians claim it is total obscenity, pure nonsense. But this refusal and destruction of the riot's language is precisely the content of its most central act: looting.

Looting is direct action par excellence. Looters attack their enemies and exploiters while improving the lives of those who participate in the action.

But it is also a nearly irrecuperable aesthetic gesture against the police, whiteness, and the regime of property that gives those forces power and purpose. In revealing the innately ideological and social content of property owner-ship—in demonstrating that all that stands between us and plenty is a thin sheet of plate glass—looting destabilizes the ideological hold of whiteness, property, and capital, and it has done so since the enslaved looted themselves singly and *en masse* from the plantation.

This conversation is an act of remembering these ges-tures, an attempt to clear away some of the ashes and dirt thrown by generations of reactionaries, so that the embers of liberation might once again catch tinder and alight. It has been collectively edited for clarity.

—Vicky Osterweil,
Spring 2022

Vicky Osterweil (VO) When Jose and Andreas approached me about this project, they asked me who would be on my dream panel, and it was you three. So it's a huge honor that we were all able to gather and have this conversation. We're here to talk about "looting." It's a framing theme that follows from the book I wrote, *In Defense of Looting*.[2] You've all touched on the topic in your work, through questions about property, resistance, and liberation, particularly as it relates to black struggle and history. It's really exciting to be able to talk about 2020 and struggle after these years of counterrevolution that I think have been very, very difficult.

Looting, alongside street fighting with the police and attacks on police property, particularly their vehicles and their precincts, was among the core tactics of the George Floyd rebellion, certainly during the first two weeks when it was really at its height. There haven't been a lot of reflections on this aspect of the uprising, but even in the ones that have emerged there has not been that much attention to the attack on property as a core moment in the struggle. Understandably, people focus on the police and police violence, but I think there is something about looting, and attacks on property in general, that is sort of opaque and unspeakable, even to people who are on the side of liberation and revolution. I would love for us to think about what makes people squeamish about attacks on property and what makes those acts so frightening to the powers that be—so frightening in fact that some city governments said that they were going to abolish their police just to try and get people to stop looting and off the streets.

Rinaldo Walcott (RW) Yes, I think you're correct that there has not been a lot of reflection on the George Floyd murder and communities' responses in Minnesota, in the "post-revolutionary moment," as you correctly name it, nor about how, during this potential revolutionary moment, the pushback against "defund the police" encapsulates that problem. I'm going to come back to that, but for myself, when I wrote about looting in my own work, I was thinking very much about arguments that I was exposed to and trained around as a student. For a significant part of my undergraduate education, we spent a lot of time reading the work of Eugene Genovese, his *Roll, Jordan, Roll*, thinking about and debating the question of what constitutes slave resistance and the worlds that the slaves made.[3] And of course, a part of resistance was always in the small rebellions, the breaking of tools, the poisoning of masters, the sabotaging of crops, and so on. For me, this kind of question about looting is a part of that tradition. Black looting in the moment of resistance, in the moment of refusal, in the moment of rebellion, becomes a part of that longer tradition in which this is not a practice where black people simply want to have access to commodities and material goods. But actually, it's a sense of a really deep dissatisfaction with what those things mean.

At the same time, it's an act of survival. When we look at what black people take when they "loot," it's usually food items, medications, and so on. Of course, the media always finds the person with the big, flat-screen TV. This tells us something about how this practice is about refusal and survival. In my work, I also point to how looting is part of the revolutionary process, that looting is seizing things, whether we call them commodities or other kinds of things that have been unfairly usurped. For me, there's the image of the burning police station in Minnesota. But there's also the image of the snipers on rooftops during Katrina, in New Orleans, when black people were trying to get sustenance to make it through, and those two things are, for me, really, as Christina would say, in juxtaposition in terms of how we might think about what looting is, what it represents, and how that forms the basis of black resistance and refusal.

Saidiya Hartman (SH) It is interesting to start with Genovese, especially because the left's problem with looting has to do with a particular narrative and "emplotment" of the political. Even as Genovese documents minor modalities of challenging the plantation order, they are, after all, minor modalities, and, he would say, already folded into the reproductive logic of the plantation, already anticipated and accounted for. I think looting raises the question of what defines the political? How do we imagine it? And do we aspire to have action that is legible within a certain framework of legitimacy? At the same time, a Marxist critique of looting attributes failure of the revolutionary project to black folks, slum dwellers, the dispossessed and remaindered, for not adhering to orthodox forms of political actions or legible principles. No party and no plan become the focus of the critique.

One historical example of looting that I love is the blackout in New York City in 1977. Young people stole sound systems, and those sound systems then became an integral part of the making of the new music that became rap and hip hop. A turntable is a nonessential good, and yet it is critical in the making of an expressive form that is antagonistic to order. An act of theft provides the means for expression. I know that, in different ways, all of us tend to the modes of black social life or practices of living and survival that are antagonistic to this racialized enclosure, to capitalism, to this anti-black order. In *Wayward Lives* there is a chapter in praise of the riot, in praise of tumult and upheaval, in praise of creative destruction.[4] It is legible speech, even as people like Martin Luther King said, it is the language of the unheard. There's something about its frontality—its beautifully clear articulation of not being beholden to or revering the terms of value that organize social life—that is so important to me. And it's so, so clear.

In the context of 2020, I remember one activist saying that looting is a clear sign that we're not a part of the social contract that was built on the backs of enslaved people and colonized people. Rioting is an articulation of our position outside the order. In short, we are the governed, we are not citizens. Of course, what is frightening about looting is that articulations of black antagonism can't be assimilated or framed by prevailing Western political narratives; rather, these practices jeopardize those frameworks. We need to think with people who call our attention to the limits of the political. I think that someone like Paul Gilroy tries to do this with the politics of transfiguration. In *The Undercommons*, Fred Moten and Stefano Harney essentially declare, "fuck politics."[5] Politics is a degraded category. So why then do we want to interpret black practices through that scrim? Is it a backdoor bid for recognition? To whom do we need to prove that we understand the workings of racial capitalism? Or that rioting is an articulation of antagonism?

Christina Sharpe (CS) I think I'm going to respond in a slightly different direction because, as Rinaldo and Saidiya were talking, I kept thinking about another kind of looting, the kind that those in power practice. I'm thinking about the enormous display of looting that's going on right now in England.[6] At the same time that this is going on, I'm thinking about how many people in the UK are worried that they're not going to make it through the winter in terms of heating. Their wages and their social insurance are not going to cover food, housing, and heating costs. They're really struggling to figure out how they're going to make this inadequate amount of money stretch. And then there is this funeral for the Queen, these nineteen days of show that cost six billion pounds or something. So, I'm thinking about the kind of looting that the Crown is doing to maintain that which they acquired through looting while a huge majority of people are utterly impoverished. 70 percent of people in England will not be able to pay for their heating this winter, by some accounts.[7] That form of looting is not called looting. I'm thinking about an article I read in *Hyperallergic* about the extent to which US museums will go to hide what they acquired through looting.[8] And so what's legible as looting, and looting as practice, is what Canada and the US are founded on. And that made me think of two books: Anna Julia Cooper's *A Voice from the South* and Charles Waddell Chesnutt's *The Marrow of Tradition*. In the former, Cooper is thinking about the ways in which a certain kind of looting was respectable when you get far enough from it. She writes:

Then, too, the South represented blood—not red blood, but blue blood. The difference is in the length of the stream and your distance from its source. If your own father was a pirate, a robber, a murderer, his hands are dyed in red blood, and you don't say very much about it. But if your great great great grandfather's grandfather stole and pillaged and slew, and you can prove it, your blood has become blue and you are at great pains to establish the relationship.[9]

Here you can see a different relationship to looting and how one becomes aristocracy through its practice. This is more of a sideways response to these questions surrounding legibility, power, narrative, aesthetics, and respectability.

SH Christina, that's a brilliant point. I too read the article in *Hyperallergic* in which David Frum [George W. Bush's speechwriter] argues that the Benin bronzes should not be returned. Of course, it's intimately connected with the "inability of Africans to govern themselves." This sentiment is at the heart of colonial discourse. We have a term for that kind of looting and it's called *accumulation* or *conservation*. So what does it mean to think about accumulation, whether original or "primitive," in relation to looting or rioting, which is nothing more than a bare-bones descriptor of the radical, critical imaginings of the wretched and the dispossessed? Where is the robust left analytic that extends this thought in deed? We don't call accumulation looting or theft because we have other language for it: the historical conditions for the reproduction of capitalism. Without such an analytic, we continue to distinguish between these two orders—accumulation and looting—and therefore treat them as if they aren't intimately entangled. One of the things that you, Vicky, write in your book is that there's so-called "good" looting and "bad" looting, where "good" looting is taking/acquiring food, medicine, or bread. But, you know . . . don't steal Yeezys.

CS Or the 62-inch TV.

[*Everybody laughs.*]

SH Right! Exactly. Because then you're just a bad consumer. And I think this really goes to your point, Christina. Why are there not masses of people in the streets making the Queen's funeral impossible?

CS Absolutely. There are miles of people waiting to see that wretched woman.

SH Moreover, and as Stephanie Smallwood writes in *Saltwater Slavery*, both the slave ship as well as slavery as a whole provided a laboratory for testing the limits to which life can be pushed: a laboratory of managed depletion.[10] Questions regarding the minimal standards for the social reproduction of the poor, the unhoused, and the working class are issues to which there is a surprising degree of agreement across the political spectrum. Given this consensus, some actions, like "bad" looting, appear to be going "too far." Therefore, "bad" looting is not "politics," but rather a form of consumption, generated by the logic and desires of capital rather than opposed to it. In part, this is because the assumptions about what is essential to social reproduction are shared and taken for granted.

I'm also thinking here about the space of the settler colony—the US, Canada, and South Africa—and the intensity, immediacy, and directness of violence in the racial state and the settler order. Recently, there was an article in *The New York Times* reporting that 40 percent of the blood plasma in Europe is imported from the US, because the US is the only country in which it's accepted that poor people can sell their plasma for money.[11] How do we exist in this state? It's so, so brutal. People donate plasma, and the process takes about four hours. They receive $35. To prevent people from doing it twice in one day, they mark people's fingernails so they can't go to another blood plasma donation center. So, people who are literally forced to sell their blood now remove their fingernails so they can donate to a second center. So, there is a new rule that if you're missing a fingernail, you can't donate plasma. What is the order that requires people to sell their blood, their organs, their reproductive capacities to survive?

Meanwhile, there's a six-billion-pound spectacle celebrating the British empire, and all of the major Western media outlets are praising the "order and stability" of the Queen's reign. Order and stability are euphemisms for terror, imperialism, colonialism, and the racial order. The West absolutely celebrates and utterly affirms it. Looting reveals the cleavage in our political imaginaries. Our needs and wants, our visions of the planet are utterly incommensurable, resolutely antagonistic. The discourse of Anthropocene can't hide or suture that. This is the hard truth articulated at the site of the riot, in the act of looting. There are those people who hoped to marshal the unruly assemblies and movements of the multitude and the wretched into a politics of recognition or achieve state power and build a "good" state. But then there are those of us who say, "No, we want none of this." There is no rehabilitation possible, so all the work is focused on destitution and abolition. Most people are unwilling to go there.

RW That's really great, Saidiya. As soon as you both spoke, I started thinking about Bob Marley's "Burning and Looting." When you concluded, Saidiya, with the sense that there's no resolution, I thought about how that song also doesn't have a resolution. The two moments of affect are about praying and crying. But the kind of burning and looting that's at the center of it are responses to racial capitalism. What troubles many people about looting is that it puts that which constitutes political violence front and center. I think that the three of us would say that what's taking place since last Thursday in England is a form of political violence. But we're supposed to pretend that it's not. And, you know, the same kind of looting that we saw when Mark Duggan was killed in the UK in 2011, or that we saw in Minnesota in 2020, and that we saw in US cities in the moment of Black Power and civil rights in the '60s and '70s, and at other points in the UK in the '70s and the '80s, and for one brief moment in Toronto in 1992: that kind of political violence that both the left (the imagined white left) and liberals literally have no language or grammar to understand as responses to racial capitalism and political refusal. And so, the only way this left can make sense of it is to spectacularize it while also denying it as any form of political speech, so that they can reassimilate it into a narrative of bad behavior, of outrageous behavior, of practices that should be viewed as anathema.

Since the death of the Queen, we've been inundated with a form of political violence for which, in Canada, where I live, and in the Canadian media, there's been very, very little opening for an alternative rhetoric of the mildest kind of Republicanism—it's been entirely shut down. What I'm animated by is thinking of looting as a particular form of political speech. And a political speech that's not assimilable to the forms of speech that are already available to us. But nonetheless, it's a form of speech that does not allow us to ignore it, right? So once it occurs, one sees that the status quo finds itself in emergency, and it then begins to trot out a whole range of means of responding. And, of course, during this moment in 2020, the response was diversity, equity, inclusion (DEI). The response was the narratives of representation. But that in and of itself is not a direct response to a form of political speech that, as Marley suggests in "Burning and Looting," seeks to undo the entire system.

SH I want to add a note. Rinaldo, you're right. The media has essentially been praising monarchy. But even with glorious Republicanism, the division between the citizen and the racialized is established. Representative democracies build the plantation, the reservation, the factory, the colony, the prison. For me, the point is that statecraft is a modality of violence. That's what we see, even though it's a monarchist variant.

CS Thinking in agreement with Rinaldo and Saidiya about the fact that statecraft is a form of violence, I began to consider the different ways to conceive of this form of violence through unfathomable numbers: e.g., thirty-five million people in Pakistan unhoused because of flooding. The population of Canada is thirty-five million people . . . the entire country. So what is the possible response to this state of affairs? There's no response to this except for looting. The state is unwilling, or incapable, of actually caring for people. We have to take it all back. Whatever that means. If we don't want to think about looting only in terms of black people in the context of North America, so much of the conversation about it, even by people who are on the left, hinges on the question of respectability. As Saidiya said, the distinction between "good" looting and "bad" looting is a distinction *without a difference.* In light of everything that we face, it seems to me that looting is the only answer.

RW Christina, that makes me think of something. Following from the distinction between "good" and "bad" looting developed in Vicky's work and that you and Saidiya have alluded to, is the question: where does "good" looting sit?

The museum is a monument to "good" looting, even in its moment of claiming to be reckoning with the return of various objects and so on. So it's okay for US museums to return objects to Greece or even for the British Museum to return objects to Greece, but it's not okay for the British Museum, or France, or the US, or the German museum system to return objects to African nations, right? Whether it's Senegal, Nigeria, or elsewhere. Even in these new arrangements, the fine print is that they're actually *lending* these objects back to Nigeria or Senegal and so on. And that is premised on the claim that museums in the Global North have certain kinds of infrastructures that will support and enable the ongoing exhibition of all of these objects. Not to be too romantic about it, but these objects are not being reintegrated back into societies. These objects are being *lent* to where they were extracted from, along with very, very tight display, exhibition, and engagement guidelines. This is a kind of brutal extension of Europe and its own partiality, constituted in the only way that it can be: buttressed by violence.

CS This is just a small point to add. A few years ago, we had a conversation at the Canadian Centre for Architecture in Montreal and somebody in the audience asked the question about returning items to Senegal, Nigeria, or Mali, and was making the argument that these countries don't necessarily have the infrastructure to maintain the proper conditions, humidity, proper lighting, etcetera. But Venice is flooded; climate disasters are coming for everybody. So who are you, a looter, to act as caretaker of the things which you looted, which, at other times, you also burned and destroyed? So, how can these people purport to be the arbiters of care when that supposed care both continues and is premised on violence? On top of that, who's to say those objects are supposed to last into the present anyway?

SH I agree. In the [1850s Xhosa] cattle killing, Nongqawuse states: "If we have to destroy everything to get rid of the colonizer, that is what we will do." It was the vision of the Haitian revolution: we will burn the entire island down. *That* is the condition, the requirement, for freedom. And, ultimately, that's how the war is won. The discourse of civilization still asks us, "Can you tend to the objects that you have produced and created?" It is a rhetorical question. The answer is no. We do not possess the requisite skills and capacity to care for the objects that we, in fact, have produced.

I wanted to say something earlier when Rinaldo was talking about DEI, which, at the end of the day, is just neoliberal governance. After the summer of 2020 in particular, elite institutions want the black person at the table; they want the trans person at the table; they want the Indigenous person at the table; they want the differently abled person at the table; and they want them to have the same conversation they've been having for the last three hundred years. They want us there to cosign the project, to pretend that it has legitimacy.

Inclusion is a form of containment and enclosure. But actually nothing is ceded.

In light of all this, it is no surprise that we are all looters. We don't have standing to own property anyway. It is a fact. That's why we are arrested and murdered as we enter our own houses, why we are stopped as we're driving our cars. While there is a right to bear arms, we also know we don't have that right. What ultimately determines the difference between "good" and "bad" looting is this history of who has been owned and who has been property. It prevents any natural or easy relationship between black folks and property. The worldview of the bourgeoisie, the colonial scheme, the design for mastery inculcates the idea "oh, we should want that too." And even as we are solicited and seduced by it, ultimately we can't have it because we don't have the standing that would enable that kind of relationship to proceed in any easy way. The mundane example of this is the black homeowner whose home is evaluated under market value . . . .

CS . . . for hundreds of thousands of dollars less.

SH Right! So basically, to have the value of your home recognized, you have to disappear blackness and have your white neighbor stand in for you because, ultimately, they're the ones who can enhance and reproduce value. Precisely for this reason—and Rinaldo says this in his book on property as well—there is an organic antagonism between blackness and property. And that antagonism is *structural*. I love that moment in Frederick Douglass' 1855 narrative when they make the plan for the revolt inside the Freedom School. When the slave owner discovers said plan, they pass along this note which says, "Own nothing." That, for me, is an allegory of our struggle for freedom: own nothing!

CS If one has been made into property by law, then the only orientation should be looting: the orchestrated theft of oneself and others. Harriet Tubman was a looter.

RW Yes! I was going to say that it is exactly this question—how do black people own their bodies?—that is the fundamental question of looting, but understood in light of a European humanism and modernity that has also made black people into permanent squatters. We are forced to squat everywhere that we are, including in putatively black countries. There are all of these no-go places that black people must continually grapple with as they try to live their lives. And so this kind of permanent quality of being the squatter is also a demand to engage in forms of political violence that overturn all of that. Not that it brings us into a new world, even though I am one of those people who kind of rolls with the Fanonian notion of a kind of new humanism, or at least the possibility of it.

Returning to the museum, then, what they're actually saying in these repatriation agreements is that the work can squat in one of those places from where it was taken for a while. And so this raises the question Sylvia Wynter asks us to think about in her essay on aesthetics: what does aesthetics do and what does aesthetics mean, and to what extent is aesthetics meant to activate a politics, a set of political positions, right? What we see with these agreements of repatriation, and even the way in which they use the word "reparation" in relation to these questions, is that the African, the black person, must now come into the European logic of aesthetics, of a very particular understanding of what aesthetics means. And so, yes, we can't return these objects to the villages that they were looted from and have the villagers use them how they might have used them before. Here, the notion of desecration is really important for me. I believe that black people must continually desecrate modernity. We have to make sure that, in relation to these objects, the notion of desecration becomes one of the fundamental framing devices of the conversations that people are having inside museum communities regarding these objects' "return," instead of having those objects squat for a while in Senegal, or in Nigeria, or Ghana, or Benin, or what have you.

SH Of course I was thinking a lot about Sylvia Wynter too. Her article on deciphering practice offers a critical discourse on the aesthetic as part of the ontological cognitive colonizing schema of the European project. She reads a film like *The Harder They Come* (1972) as a site of this critical deciphering practice in the figure of the bandit or the rude boy. So, in one sense, that would seem to be very confluent with looting. I want to think about black sociality, because even imagining that one might live in this order requires radical thought and another conception of social living. I keep returning to Wynter's *Beyond the Categories of the Master Conception*, which is particularly related to what you said, Rinaldo.[12] Even brilliant C. L. R. James' discernment is restricted when he's thinking solely through the Marxist critical framework, right? In his novel *Minty Alley*, he attends to the space of the Caribbean through the character of Matthew Bondsman. Wynter argues that, in the novel, he is able to exceed the Marxist framework by attending to the social life of the yard—what Laura Harris terms "the aesthetic sociality of blackness." As a result, other categories come into view.[13] The key terms are accumulation and domination. It's not limited to the worker or exploitation. What comes into view is the extreme domination and the accumulation that is the precondition for the worker's exploitation.

For Wynter, it's about the text of sociality and what she calls the undercurrent or underlife of black culture. It refers to a set of dispositions that are inherently antagonistic to the limited Western worldview and that of European man one and man two, who have become so enormous as to become the sum of human philosophy, ontology, and aesthetics. The domain of lived experience and social practice are so important because they fundamentally challenge this framework. I would add looting to the larger category of everyday practices of black antagonism.

VO There's so many things to say here, but one thing just before I respond directly: when you, Rinaldo, were talking about squatting and the Queen, I was thinking about the circularity of that history. When Elizabeth II came to power, the Mau Mau Rebellion [in colonized Kenya] was kicking off: a rebellion that started as a squatters' movement. It was a movement expressed through the squatting of agricultural land. And they're squatting while she's ascending that mythical staircase or whatever.

In response to European institutions saying, "These people aren't civilized enough to hold the art," I was reminded of Iraq and how the looting and destruction of the Baghdadi Museum in 2005 is one of the greatest works of destruction and dispersal of historical artifacts ever. But this destruction was possible precisely because the US had destabilized the country. So, in a way, the claim that "you are not responsible enough to keep the art" is really saying "we can't leave the art with you, because someday we may want to invade, intervene or destabilize your country, and, as a potential target of imperial violence, we can't keep anything of true value with you."

In terms of a form of social practice, one of the things that I noticed, both in the research I was doing and from personal experience, is that the space of the riot is very joyous and playful. Of course there's lots of anger as well, and when you're at the frontline confronting the police, it's obviously very intense. But, almost exclusively that anger and intensity is focused on, by the right and the left, while the joy is downplayed or ignored.

I'm thinking about a recent example in Philly. In 2020, there was this one shop that made "untucked button downs." It is like a pop-up shop for untucked shirts, and they were so ugly, that while every other business around them had been destroyed during the rebellions, it became a shared joke that no one touched this place. If it were just about value or survival, those shirts would have been just as valuable as the stuff next door. So there's this playfulness and also an aesthetic judgment going on in those spaces of riot that can't be reduced to political or economic claims. How does it serve white supremacy to downplay or make that joy invisible?

RW I think the key is your example of the Baghdadi Museum because it really takes us back to the different qualities of what constitutes looting. Because we know that the looters didn't just destroy that museum. They looted it as well. And now the objects are circulating around Europe, among a particular kind of collector class. But I think your example from Philly is about the jouissance of the riot, the jouissance of looting. And if you've been in that moment or been really close to it, you know that there's something that happens *bodily*, when the crowd surges forward and decides to break the door and you either participate or you watch it happen. It makes me think about the subversive quality of the carnival. It makes me think about other modes of being. When Saidiya invoked the question of black sociality, I thought of how, in the part of the Caribbean where I come from, carnivals were often banned. In Barbados, where I was born, the carnival was banned from the late 1800s into the mid 1950s and then began to return in small movements. The carnival was celebrated at the end of the harvest, and partly that's because it's not a Catholic country. And so the carnival was understood to be a kind of jouissance, a kind of possibility of an uprising where the slave or the ex-slave might not return to the plantation next season. The carnival had to be contained because labor had to be contained and returned for the tilling of the soil and the new crops.

Something that has fascinated me for many years is Rastafarian culture because so many of the movements begin with a moment of squatting, a moment of black sociality where they occupy a piece of land. And that often ends up becoming a confrontation that gets labeled as a riot by the authorities. But what they've done is they've occupied something and they've tried to make a kind of communal black social form of life present and available to those who are willing and interested in joining. What I'm trying to say is that what we might call looting—not the looting of Europe, not the looting of capital, but this other thing that we call looting—is a way of giving a narrative to what those other forms of looting cannot do. Black looting is black sociality.

SH Rastafarianism is so central to the development of critical thought for Wynter and Kamau Brathwaite. When Wynter addresses the glimmerings of black sociality and what it might yield, she's thinking about Rastafarianism, right? Precisely because it is against the Order of Babylon. It is not going to participate in any way. So again there is refusal. I do not intend to confine Rastafarianism to negation, but to emphasize that negation is generative and productive. I don't think we could imagine Braithwaite's poetics without Rastafarianism, right? So I think all the points that you're making, Rinaldo, are really critical. For me, this is why the issue of practicing sociality is so important. Another one of those moments is Orlando Patterson's looking at Trenchtown and asking, "How the hell did we get here? What is the enormous violence that made all of this possible?" This leads him to theorize social death. How do we live in the context of this social death? Again, contesting the rights of ownership, withdrawing one's labor, not submitting to the script of development, not identifying as the citizen-subject. It reveals a profound understanding of the limits of politics.

RW I'm glad that you invoke Orlando Patterson because I was thinking about exactly that moment in *The Children of Sisyphus*, because Rastafari and its logics are so central to a whole other way of being. I grew up as a child in the mid 1970s, seeing Rastafarians being carted away and accused of being mentally ill because of their entire investment in not participating in the political forms that were deemed legitimate, claiming communal practices that were seen to be an anathema. And so as a child, as a ten- or eleven-year-old child, the language that I heard most often applied to Rastafarians was that they were either mad or that they were thieves. Going back to my undergraduate classes and reading Genovese, I think of the kind of debates in our classes about what constituted resistance. And of course, we also read

Patterson, and we were reading Derek Walcott, and, at that point in the 1980s, the debate in these classes was about why we don't just return to Africa or return to Europe. And often our professors were invoking Walcott as the kind of figure that sorts it out for us, right? You know, we don't have to have a divided tongue. Europe is as much a part of who we are as is Africa, and so on. In that particular moment, Braithwaite gets short shrift. Braithwaite is pushing too much, too much towards Africa. And by the '90s, in terms of my own intellectual development, I began to see Rastafari produced as this really important symbolic figure of an emergent Caribbean. For a while, that really kind of messed with my head because I was like, but no, these were the people that you reviled. I remember when I first grew dreadlocks, my mum begged me not to come visit Barbados again because she was absolutely convinced that I was going to be arrested as soon as I landed at the airport.

CS That was like me growing up outside of Philadelphia and watching MOVE, and John Africa, and the back-to-Africa movement and seeing the arrests and humiliation of MOVE members, the destruction of the MOVE House in 1978 in the Powelton Village neighborhood, and then of course on May 13, 1985, the city dropped two bombs on the MOVE house on Osage Avenue.[14] But the sort of language around those groups is similar to what you are saying: they're "stealing" from people's garbage. They're "mad." To wear dreadlocks in Philadelphia in the '80s and '90s was to be subjected to police violence. All of the language around MOVE was an attempt to make them incomprehensible, an attempt to make their commitments to communal living and self-governance completely unrecognizable. The completely negative coverage of them was also meant to enlist others in the work of surveillance. MOVE members were subjected, as we know, to all forms of violence. It's not the first black community, but it is one of the first to be bombed from the air by the state.

RW I grew my first head of dreadlocks after reading Audre Lorde's "Is Your Hair Still Political?" because it crystallized for me not just what black hair meant, but what dreadlocks meant in the context of a particular kind of aesthetic.[15] Your hair could immediately set a kind of politics for you in motion.

SH I, too, remember the way Walcott and Brathwaite were pitted against one another. Certainly, in the university, Walcott won the war. And I think that he won because of his command of the Western canon, a tradition that the black person must acknowledge and wrestle with. Walcott's incredible body of work also serves to re-enchant the ideality of the West. Walcott's elegant way of inhabiting those grand texts meant that it didn't matter if you had only six books in the library: as long as the Bible, Shakespeare, and Homer were among them, you were good, right? You had everything you needed. Brathwaite questioned all of that and explored what it meant to write in "nation language," to regard the beauty of the demotic.[16] It pushed against the values of the canon and conceived of writing as being grounded with working class folks and peasants.

One of my favorite images of looting is a photograph taken in the context of the 1935 Harlem riots. There is a long line of black women who are being arrested, but they look as if they just left church, looted, and then got caught by the police—they're wearing very nice dresses, heels, and stockings, keeping in their possession all the looted items, while the police are leading them to the paddy wagon. For me, it's a beautiful image because it's not the rude boy, and it's not the Rasta. The caption would be something like, "On my way home from church, I passed the store that has been exploiting us and won't hire us. Should I enter and take something? Absolutely!" I grew up in a black community. I remember going into the barbershop or the beauty salon with my very middle-class-striving mom, and there were always people in the shop who were selling stolen goods. Always! Everyone browsed the merchandise, "Oh, that's really good." "That's not my size. Can you get me a size ten the next time you go to Macy's?" Despite the fact that it would be the end of the world if my brother or I were to steal anything, there was an understanding that this was fine, that some people made their living this way. It reveals the complexity of the black social text. This was the cause of Du Bois' consternation and puzzlement: how are these upstanding Negroes getting along with the hoodlums? They seem to be living together in a certain kind of harmony. Why isn't there a harsh line of distinction? I believe the reason is a shared understanding of our state, a knowledge of the structural predicament.

CS Thinking about looting and black racialization, an image that has stuck with me since Katrina, a media juxtaposition of an image of an identifiably white-skinned black man "carrying" something; an image of two people, a woman and a man, "looting" groceries; and an image of another woman "finding" groceries. Every time I look at that image, you know that the woman who's finding groceries is also black. And it's a particular inability to locate her as black that then grants her absence from criminality. But she is a black woman; she has cornrows; and it's Louisiana. So I'm thinking about the absolute racialization of looting in those moments and how that becomes utterly clear in the ways in which she is passed out of the category of having stolen something into the category of finding—just like Europeans finding as opposed to stealing.

SH There's also the matter of value. We don't value what they value. There's a great Claire Denis film, *White Material* (2009). I love the scene in which the men find a gold watch and all this other "valuable stuff." They look at it and say, "white material." I thought it was such a brilliant articulation of the lack of inherent value in European prized objects. The men don't think the gold watch is precious. It's like, oh yeah, these are the kind of objects that are valued by the whites. Their disdain is expressed in labeling it as such. This contestation or incommensurability of values is critical. We witness the same phenomenon expressed differently in these scenes of looting or destitution. It's like, oh, we don't actually value this. We have no connection to this. This doesn't produce a future for us. So why should we have any attachment to it at all? This moment is really terrifying because what black people are called to do is to affirm the order, to state unequivocally, "Oh my God, we believe in this order. Its values are so great. We believe in it more than anyone else. We believe in it deeply and truly." In the riot it is clear, "No. We don't believe in it. We are content to see it burn to the ground." Our radical indifference to the national project is on display. The desire to bring about its end is revealed. The repressed and the unspeakable are in plain view. Given our experience in this order, how could we love it? How could we? Yet, the myth of social cohesion and the narratives of belonging and citizenship require that we love it as much as anyone else. We just want recognition; we just want our share. We are here to aid the survival of the order. So to say, "We don't care. We're not invested in the survival of the order," is terrifying for those who imagine us as the implements for the reproduction and enhancement of their life, value, and well-being.

CS Absolutely.

SH It's a different narrative.

CS It seems to me that this gets back to Vicky's question about joy in the riot and what, in particular, is so terrifying about looting. I always come back to Chesnutt's novel *The Marrow of Tradition* where, at first, the sight of black people daring to be well-dressed and enjoying themselves in the middle of the day enrages the white man, Major Carteret. But then it's the sound of Negro laughter that fundamentally drives him to become part of the Wellington Three, those white men who ultimately lead the 1898 Insurrection.[17] So it's not exactly that the joy of liberation is unspeakable. Rather, this joy corresponds to something about black sociality that is not paying any attention to whiteness and white people. It doesn't want what white people want, and it laughs at you with your desire, your motivation, your intention of accumulation, all of which is utterly discombobulating and terrifying. This joy is founded on the fact that we might not want what you want, that we might not want to mortgage our lives to attain that which has been part of our undoing.

RW I want to say something that all of this sparked for me just now. It has to do with this question of how, during a particular moment, Rastafari enacted a crisis of value; it turned value upside down and inaugurated a whole other way of thinking about what might be called value. And that became such a challenge to society that, of course, they had to be repressed. I think this jouissance of looting, and of the riot, is also another moment of the articulation of a different notion of value, right? The refusal of property as this thing that should be respected, the refusal of the notion that it's okay to have these places stacked with all of these commodities that people actually need for their everyday lives, and that a protest would just walk by them as if they're not there for the taking. And one of the things that modern societies simply cannot grapple with is when we begin to articulate values that are not within the authorized normative logic. You will see the status quo at its most brutal and violent when that happens. And so the counterrevolution to 2020 was to use these practices of DEI to incorporate people into the moral and economic value systems of the status quo, without even reforming. It was not even a reformist project. It was simply a project of incorporation. Incorporation into the museum, or the art gallery, or the university . . . .

CS . . . into publishing, Netflix, into every industry. It is now a process of injection. Rinaldo, it's what you call the "George Floyd dividend." People mistook individual advancement for something like an undoing and a remaking of how these institutions might work.

SH I remember when in the summer of 2020, one of the founders of BLM basically said, "We've arrived." I couldn't believe it. Just because of the currency of defunding the police as political rhetoric? What we now know is that the rhetoric of defunding the police produced enormous material dividends for the police! In NYC, we have a cop for mayor. This is where my own agnosticism regarding politics becomes prominent. What does it mean to be involved in a form of radical organizing that then becomes legible as politics with policy recommendations, political endorsements, etc., as opposed to the forms of destitution which sustain us and are key to the protracted struggle against racial capitalism and anti-blackness? I had a friend who attempted to create an intentional radical community by buying houses and by helping people who were living in substandard housing to improve their dwellings. The moment in which it registered as value-making, developers swept in and totally undermined the whole project. I was talking with this friend, someone in real estate, about the Invisible Committee and their project of destitution and her response was, "I absolutely agree." After the demise of the project, they accepted and understood that we shouldn't be trying to build property holdings or develop anything. That is not the way to sustain community, because the moment we create any value is the moment of gentrification and appropriation. So what does it mean to embrace destitution in a way that's enabling?

I'm not saying that there is no work to do that's educational and pedagogical. But I do feel that 95 percent of antiracist work needs to be done by white people who are dedicated to the project of abolishing whiteness. We need to be involved in projects that make the unbearable sustainable, that enhance survival in a context in which we're not supposed to live, a world in which we're not supposed to thrive. So what might we do instead of being involved in these "grand" projects of addressing the white world and educating those devoted to maintaining their innocence, while they monopolize the earth and public resources. I would like us to refuse participating in those kinds of activities, which are exhausting and yet change very little.

RW I think the example you gave, Saidiya, is a really good one for what I mean when I say that black people have been forced to be squatters of this earth. At any moment that black people are able to be associated with the reproduction of racial capital and its values, they also get pushed out. So we both generate it and are representative of the problem of it. What if destitution becomes the ground that we defend? Not because there's something sacred in destitution. But how can we reanimate destitution as the site for a different kind of politics? And, in some ways, that's what Patterson was trying to get at in *The Children of Sisyphus* in that brief moment of his radicality.

SH I really like that formulation. It conveys the imagination of ex-slaves and fugitives. They wanted to escape the plantation order. They did not want to be conscripted as wage laborers, but they were forced to sign contracts as sharecroppers. In the South, all other means of subsistence were criminalized. You couldn't hunt. You couldn't fish. You could not pursue any activities that would enable you to sustain yourself outside of wage labor. It made survival impossible. The intensity and scope of violence was necessary to create wage laborers. You have to totally cut out all possibilities of surviving outside of wage labor. For me, destitution also embraces other values, other visions of life and survival, especially the notion of living on just enough.

The other great example is fugitive ecological practices. What was required to reside in transient zones of freedom? Some people might call them temporary autonomous zones, which are near the plantation, and not like the hills in Jamaica. One is required to dwell and exist without leaving any signs of human habitation because if you leave any signs, then the patrollers and the master can find you. These practices model other ways of inhabiting Earth that are not about development or fences, or acquisition or privatization or intensive farming. It is so important to attend to the matter of practice because there's just so much brilliance entailed in navigating everyday life. How is it that we can survive without repro-ducing the terms of the dominant order?

CS This reminds me of three things. Firstly, the Great Dismal Swamp, where there are remains of maroon commu-nities where many people were sure that no one could sur-vive because the conditions were so harsh. But for decades, people lived in those swamps. We know because of the things that people have found buried there. They lived there in ways that were undetectable. And so to live in that harshness and to survive, to reproduce, and to keep each other safe is one thing. The second thing that I'm thinking of here is that sen-tence, "They owe, own nothing," which comes to me from "Ruttier for the Marooned in the Diaspora" in Dionne Brand's *A Map to the Door of No Return: Notes to Belonging*. Third, I was thinking about the testimony of the formerly enslaved man named Fountain Hughes, who is 101 years old when he is interviewed. In the interview he spends a long time talking about how he doesn't owe anybody any money, and he never bought anything on credit. And it's so clear that he's going on and on about this because, of course, he has been an object, property, that could be traded, that could be repossessed. So he is committed to not reproducing that order, and that's why he spends many minutes of this interview talking about what it means to live a certain kind of debt-free life. This kind of destitution, which is something other than destitution in the order of the West, is another way of thinking about how one might survive in relation to other people, a kind of lateral understanding of what we must make, what we do make, how we might survive without reproducing the order that enslaved us. There's this incredible moment in the interview where the white man interviewing him, who I think is a descendent of slave owners, says to him, "How about you, Uncle Fountain, would you rather be a slave again?" And then, really quietly, Fountain Hughes replies, "Let me tell you, if I found out I was ever going to be a slave again, I'd go right now and I would shoot myself because then you're nothing but a dog."

SH I'm a native New Yorker, and last night I was in a taxi crossing 125th Street. I don't know, I've probably crossed 125th Street a thousand times. I remembered when I was a child in the car with my dad, I'd look out the window at the painted storefronts. A Panamanian artist had painted virtually all of the grills on the stores on 125th Street. And no matter how late it was, the streets were crowded, people were out. I loved the painted landscapes, and, of course, the gates were installed to prevent people from looting or breaking the glass windows, but they beautified the stores with lovely scenes. When I rolled through last night, all I saw was big box stores and luxury housing or big craters in the earth where luxury housing would be built. Moreover, there was no one on the street. It was 9:00 PM, and I thought, "Wow, all the people are gone." All the people who used to reside in Harlem have been moved out. They've been forced out. Blocks of multimillion-dollar apartments have been built. And this is what? The "improvement" of Harlem? The "development" of Harlem? It made me so sad because I have so many memories of those streets. My brother and I were always on the lookout for some crazy stuff happening on 125th Street. And now, there's nothing.

CS In Toronto, you see all the brutal force brought to bear on people who were living in encampments. The police came in to evict them and said nobody could come in there, and then you saw film crews show up a couple of weeks later after it had been done. At the same time, I keep thinking about the same house that's been replicated again and again. So you buy a house for one-and-a-half million dollars that, ten years ago, was 200,000 dollars. You completely destroy it. Sometimes you destroy the whole thing and you build a new thing. It's three floors. It's got big windows in it. It's the same house again and again and again. And I keep thinking, wow, these people really think they're safe. With the numbers of unhoused people, the kind of incipient rage you feel on the streets, it just makes me wonder how these people can feel so safe. These houses are monuments to what they think is their brilliance, monuments to their "success," to their being able to navigate this savage system.

SH They believe they're sovereign.

RW Which is why they can take to the streets in commemoration and mourning for Elizabeth II, right? The identification is that we are all these little sovereigns. The extension of this kind of question of the problem of value for black people and black life made me think about the recent Billie Holiday documentary, *Billie* (2020). Toward the end of that documentary, they talk about Billie dying in hospital and having 750 dollars in her bank account. Earlier in the movie, she talks about writing "God Bless the Child" as a response to her mother, who she had asked for some money. Her mother had said no. And so Billie writes this song as a kind of response to that rejection. But then her own financial life becomes caught up between her last husband and the white manager who apparently colluded with the FBI to continually get her arrested for drug possession. At the moment that she's about to die, literally handcuffed in bed in the hospital, the husband becomes the executor; he inherits her work and future money! This got me thinking about the work of destitution and how the radical position for black people cannot be one of accumulation, cannot be one of a logic of economic inheritance. In that sense, I'm also thinking about the problem of reparations, especially when reparations are constructed through a narrative of generational wealth, and that reparations will somehow create a foundation for black people to engage in the project of accumulation, the project of inheritance, of financial inheritance, and so on. We were already the site of the financialization of the body. And I don't know if there's anything much more that we can do to resist than inherit the radical process of destitution. And maybe the radical project of destitution is what might save this Earth too. So thank you for putting that on the table, Saidiya.

VO As you were talking about the ecology of destitution and a healing, destituent ecology, I was reminded of this quote from the end of Butch Lee's biography of Harriet Tubman, *Jailbreak out of History* (2021). A reporter comes to interview Tubman at her home. She's in her nineties at this point:

> When years later, in her old age, a reporter for the *New York Herald Tribune* came to interview her one afternoon at her home in Auburn, he wrote that, as he was leaving, Harriet looked towards an orchard nearby and said, "Do you like apples?" On being assured that the young man liked them, she asked, "Did you ever plant any apples?" The writer confessed that he had not. "No," said the old woman, "but somebody else planted them. I liked apples when I was young. And I said, 'Someday I'll plant apples myself for other young folks to eat.' And I guess I did."[18]

RW What can you say after that?

CS That sounds like a good place to end.

VO Thank you all so much. I'm so honored.

CS It's always a pleasure.

RW Thank you. Thank you. A pleasure, absolutely.

SH Great to see you. Great to meet you.

CONCLUSION: THINKING WITH MARINA

Andreas Petrossiants and Jose Rosales

Though Marina Vishmidt was not able to join for the roundtable conversations that were printed as *Diversity of Aesthetics*, the project has been deeply indebted to her work from the very beginning and has benefitted from her comradely involvement. On March 13, 2024, Marina joined Jose Rosales and Olia Sosnovskaya to discuss *Looting* at the Academy of Fine Arts Vienna. After Jose presented the discussions from the three volumes of the project and offered remarks building from *Looting* to discuss the ongoing genocide of the Palestinians by Israel (some of which have been included in the introduction to this book), Marina offered several generative and trenchant questions for consideration. Here, we present her comments from the Vienna event and provide some thoughts in response. As with all of Marina's work, her incisive critique about all that exists on the level of the infrastructure will continue prompting us to respond for many years to come.

Marina Vishmidt I'm very interested in the formulation that you use as the core idea of the [third] volume: "looting is the theft of property that no longer presupposes the property-form." From this standpoint, the restoration of property relations is counterrevolution in a nutshell. At the same time, [the participants of the conversation in Volume 3 make clear that] looting is just one of a series of practices, perhaps an exemplary one, of what it would take to both materially and politically challenge a society constructed around the property-form and that variant of the property-form that is waged labor. It is, as Rinaldo Walcott says, "revolutionary practice." But I was wondering whether it's also a prefigurative practice. What are the practices and temporalities for prefiguration that it makes possible? For Saidiya Hartman, for example, it could be a way for getting the means of social reproduction and even culture into our own hands, as with the New York City blackout and the birth of hip hop in the 1970s Bronx. This seems closer to a way of removing looted objects or activities of looting from property relations altogether, or into the register of "it's not that I want to claim something like *my property* back," but rather that "property has no place here." This is something which connects perhaps to some North American Indigenous epistemologies. So, is looting, then, just the post-property form of theft that can liberate its practitioners and objects from the social relation of property, per se, which "theft" describes another version of?

As Vicky Osterweil says in her discussion of the moralization of looting in her book, or rather, the "making you moral" of looting, and as Hartman brings up so eloquently in the conversation as well: when they do it, it's capitalism, or conservation, or development, or what have you, but when we do it, it's looting. There's a slight elision of what the "it" is or could be because, of course, scale and systematicity have an enormous role to play. Otherwise, the question of exploitation—whether by race, gender, class—that can differentiate and inscribe the value-form as a structural question would not make sense. Capitalism, through its dynamics, is responsible for large-scale theft and murder of the human and nonhuman world, as well as for organizing the oppression by the state and its agencies, the police, and military. So then, how do you see the problem of scale in determining what looting can be as an autonomous force, and not just a reaction to its capitalist scale [which is the] accumulation of value and the enforcement of property? We can also apply this to the designation of "riot" by police and media and how that gets turned into "law enforcement" when the same actions are undertaken by the police in relation to crowds or groups in the street. Joshua Clover has of course written extensively on the autonomous and conjunctural dimensions of the riot, as has Hartman in *Wayward Lives*—which brings me to the second question. Does looting have the riot as its precondition? Is small-scale looting just sheepish shoplifting or "stealing," easier to pigeonhole as individual deviance and disorder? And is a larger-scale attack on property outside the frame of the riot harder to inscribe into the political semiotic, such as the drugstore shoplifting that was making the news a while ago, which is an interesting chapter in the afterlife of the rebellion?

Andreas Petrossiants and Jose Rosales To begin addressing Marina's first question about prefiguration, we're thinking about how tactics of survival, expressions of militant joy, or mass "non-accumulative" social practice can directly contest the capitalist mode of production without playing by the rules of sanctioned resistance or opposition. Such actions can certainly be prefigurative in that they temporarily actualize a different mode of sociality, as well as alternative infrastructures of production, distribution, care, and so on. And, as the panelists discuss in Volume 3, non-accumulative social practices pre-exist moments of uprising and can and do inform the rhythms of moments of rebellion. This is not to accept a liberal periodization of history, but rather to insist on the timelessness of collective liberation, or rather the new temporalities produced during moments of rebellion—all the way from the "food riots" in medieval Europe to Minneapolis in 2020. In other words, the distinction between "taking *my* property back" and "property has no place here" is, among other things, a temporal one—like the "nonsynchronism" between different classes as discussed by Ernst Bloch. Looting can be one way to actualize the counter-temporality of owing and owning nothing that Christina Sharpe invokes from Dionne Brand's *A Map to the Door of No Return.*

If prefiguration, per Carl Boggs, typically assumes a certain reproducibility of forms of planning and culture for a time to come, perhaps a way to bring such a framework into conversation with spontaneity and a rejection of formalism, we can consider how the ZAD's Mauvaise Troupe Collective emphasizes "tact" rather than "tactics."[1] More recently, Kristin Ross has approached such forms of collective, non-accumulative living and action through the notion of what she calls the "commune form," or the production of a space-time that is "anchored in the art and organization of everyday life and in a collective and individual responsibility taken for the means of subsistence."[2] Ross brings in Maria Mies and Veronika Bennholdt-Thomsen's notion of the "subsistence perspective" to talk about how nonindustrial workers (peasants and farmers in particular) participate in revolutionary movements, and indeed the special fact of "their not being completely subordinated to market relations [as] an opening, a potentiality, a regeneration."[3] By operating in a nonsynchronous temporality from the advanced capitalist mode of production, alternate spaces and temporalities emerge in and through the organization of collective life. Ross continues: "Simply by clashing with the present and the concerns of the present, the outmodedness of the residual can metamorphosize into the 'emergent.'"[4] Perhaps, it is precisely looting's insistence on survival (which by definition can only be collective) and a rejection of the forms of social enclosure (e.g., the wage-form), there is the prefiguration or emergence not only of alternate property relations, which approach or even inaugurate the end of the property-form in a certain territory and time, but also the conditions for alternate relations of organization in a different time.[5] A clear example would be how in Minneapolis in 2020, looted goods were shared and distributed along mutualist networks that were set up spontaneously but addressed long-standing needs, wants, and so on.

The participants of Volume 3 consider how looting is an example of destituent insurrection or power, which similarly rejects capitalist subjectivity that is interpellated via the wage-form. As Marina reminds us, the wage is a particular appearance of the property-form, and as argued by autonomist feminists, with whose work Marina was deeply engaged, unpaid (reproductive) labor is mediated by the wage nonetheless—the "patriarchy of the wage," in Silvia Federici's phrasing. This is to say, maybe the prefigurative power of looting is contained in the replacing of the wage-relation with a "subsistence perspective," whether or not those in the square or the forest encampment arrived as waged workers or not. As Marina points out, there are limits to this formulation: even if struggles at the site of circulation (or reproduction for that matter) are inherently related to the wage, one could also say that the looted object, even once decommodified, could still fulfill the commodity's role as mediator of capitalist social relations—alienation in particular.

This comparison between looting and subsistence as potentially prefigurative is just one of the many paths Marina's first question encourages us to follow. Another direction is to interrogate the ostensible difference between an act of survival that is done under the banner of some sort of political project as opposed to an act (seemingly) divorced from such concerns. Marina is pushing us to get beyond the underlying assumptions that guarantee the reproduction of that dyad (mirrored in others like productivist versus non-productivist, social versus economic) endowed by the metaphysical assumption that actions must follow pre-existing contemplation. One way to consider this rests in realizing that all positive critique has some negativity in it and vice versa—an understanding which can be the precondition for moving towards what Marina calls an "activated negativity" that comes "from thinking how self-abolition can be grounded in some kind of material context, and how it can be a determinate rather than an abstract prescription."[6] Thus, the question of abolition is incomplete when focusing solely on the subject or object of abolition—"perhaps just liberation rather than abolition," Marina says—unless we also think about the collective process involved in abolishing the relations enforced by those objects and subject-formations. "Which is to say," she continues, "our attention is drawn to the proliferation of mediations in the process of reinventing social relations, rather than only to the destruction of existing ones implied by abolition, which might leave us with an impoverished concept of non-capitalist life."[7] And elsewhere: "Today, the valorization process can shift from forced labor to self-branding and back, and capital becomes ever more 'humanized' in proportion to its capacity to destroy all life."[8] Thus, if there is something prefigurative about looting, perhaps it is in sketching part of the process of abolition that continues past any single action or series of actions. While looting presents instances in which individuals construct new relations that afford them a greater degree of freedom in satisfying their social and material needs, such practices cannot wholly resemble the measures of abolition, or communism in other words, unless the processes of devalorization, desubjectivization, and disidentification continue to abolish the relations reproduced by whatever object or subject is being abolished in the first place. Indeed, by thinking about the everyday (where consumption is located), as Kristin Ross reminds us, we can get behind the subject/object split so integral to postwar continental philosophy.

Ross argues that movements that defend a territory and produce space can actualize a "transvaluation of value," which becomes especially evident in her analysis of the difference between resistance and defense. While the common use of the term "resistance," as in liberal resistance to the right contains the implication that "the battle is already over" and that the only mode of perseverance is to resist, defense "is grounded in a temporality and a set of priorities generated by the local community-in-the-making."[9] This is a different kind of prefiguration than that aimed at by Marxist synthesis and totality, that "has nothing to do with a demand for fairer distribution." Rather:

> The designation as *worth defending* of something that, in the existing hierarchy of value, previously had little or no value calls into question the very criteria we use for measuring or experiencing prosperity; it is a revolution of what counts as wealth, what well-being looks and feels like. It recasts what truly counts for the community-in-the-making—what it is willing to defend.[10]

Marina provides another language for this active defense in her rearticulation of "maintenance" as not just reproductive, but a something that can inhabit alienation (in relation to objects and to each other) in the direction of care—and against the individualizing precepts to notions of survival proffered by contemporary capitalism.

If looting can be considered prefigurative, perhaps it is in the way that the Black Panther Breakfast Program was prefigurative, or in the way that those fighting against the construction of Cop City in Atlanta today prefigure other modes of living with and in the forest both now and in the future: a transvaluation of exchange value into other shared values rooted in the collective. In this sense, such prefiguration might even operate like Jose Muñoz's queer worldmaking which he theorized through C. L. R. James' antiproductivist Marxism, or like the type of critical negative speculation that Marina worked so hard to wrest back from those who speculate on the future to render it the same as the present. As Marina wrote:

> The omnipresence of the future as resilient present can be equated to being cut off from having any role in the future. Being cut off from having a role in the future is nothing more or less than being cut off from having a role in the present, i.e. from social and political power. In response to this predicament, the directive often comes that "we" need to recapture the future or invent it. On the other hand, perhaps a more effective response, which

takes the fear of the future as a general affect and inverts it, is to see what it is about the present that is blocking the future . . . . Thus perhaps it can be proposed instead that thinking about the future should rather be about how to change the circumstances of the present so that futures become possible and thinkable. Perhaps then the future appears as not so much a time or a state than a dynamic of (violent) separation.[11]

Contrary to the reactionary futurisms that are speculated on by power on and around us, a prefigurative worldbuilding of the kind we are speculating on here is the motor of M. E. O'Brien and Eman Abdelhadi's 2022 novel *Everything for Everyone*.[12] The book takes place in a future in which popular rebellions have brought about postcapitalist worlds: commodities and the state have not only been abolished in many parts of the planet but have been entirely forgotten by the young; successful anticolonial struggles have liberated Palestine and parts of the Americas; cities across the world are transformed into confederations of communes that center collective empowerment and flourishing. Importantly, however, their documentation of a potential future evades the utopia/dystopia binary that would reproduce present logics of dispossession and present spatialization. In this non-capitalist reality—where much of the world thrives without wage slavery, overproduction, or continued genocide—the climate is nonetheless a disaster, organizational disagreements and harm require conflict resolution. That's what a non-accumulative future might look like: one that does not idealistically promote someone's utopia at the expense of another's, but that understands abolition as a slow process of collective action. It is not incidental that in many of the future contexts speculated on in the novel, looting was a key action in actualizing these futures.

Our invocation of fiction points to the creative and poetic dimensions of looting discussed in Volume 3 and invoked by Marina. To decommodify objects and relations reminds people that if they didn't have to spend their life toiling for wages, they might have time for other, more interesting activities, whether writing a novel or building a non-accumulative future and everything in between. One only need think of the *jouissance* that the riot allows to bloom through collective realizations of being free, as Rinaldo Walcott and Vicky Osterweil discuss in Volume 3. Another poetic exploration of this creative dimension is found in Nanni Balestrini's *Blackout*, which brings the 1977 New York blackout into relief against the late 1970s in Italy, where a decade of country-wide labor militancy was closed with severe government repression against radicals, intellectuals, workers, artists, and students at levels not seen since the fascist period. For Balestrini, the confluence of the two contexts indicated the shift to a new composition or rather decomposition of labor, for which the terms and forms of struggle would have to change. And thus, his method of poetic composition changed as well. Balestrini selected found text from disparate sources that included newspaper articles about the blackout, tourist guides for Mont Blanc, radical theory speaking to post-1968 movements, testimony from Italian militants facing charges, and pop music lyrics. He then laid out the sources on a patchwork quilt from which he chose the order and position of the texts, weaving different political and geographic contexts to narrate struggles for liberation in a stream of language and references. Because of this combination of sources, the scenes of the 1977 mass looting cease to be just a spontaneous moment of revolutionary joy, but rather the very substrate of a revolutionary everyday:

> After a few minutes the night was illuminated by fires the streets invaded by looters . . . we're going to take what we want and what we want is what we need . . . a fifty-year-old woman with a shopping bag enters a store saying today she shops for free.[13]

Balestrini, like Hartman, Walcott, Osterweil, Sharpe, and Marina, emphasizes the joy and aesthetic creativity that can emerge in such a moment of non-accumulative action, where the wage-form is no longer a barrier to self-fulfillment:

> a young man with two saxophones stopped me and said five years ago in Brooklyn I had to pawn my sax now I'll start playing again.

Here again Ross' writing on the commune-form provides helpful language. Working from Henri Lefebvre's rearticulation of Marx's theory of appropriation, Ross writes, "Appropriation implies 'usage,' rather than ownership; something like a 'right to usage' in conjunction with a right to making, or *poesis* in the broad sense of immanent social creativity, a making and a usage that ignores the legal and spatial division of mine and yours."[14] That collective appropriation, of the saxophones, of the recording equipment, of oneself, can only be non-accumulative processes explains why looting cannot be scaled without becoming something else; a non-accumulative process like looting "stands in sharp conflict with exchange because it implies appropriation and not property."[15]

To continue to bring together the questions of prefiguration and scale, we are reminded of Stefano Harney and Fred Moten's line: "scaling up is really scaling down, losing connection rather than gaining it, losing abilities rather than consolidating them, settling for form rather than formation."[16] What then are these abilities and connections that are lost when the purpose or drive of some action is to scale up? What separates the act of "sheepish shoplifting," as Marina asks, from the action's mass expression during a riot? As Marina questions the notion "when they do it, it's capitalism, or conservation, or development, or what have you, but when we do it, it's looting," what is it about this "it" that makes it resistant to being scaled, or formalized? Is the only thing separating the two examples (mass looting or "sheepish shoplifting") the number of people involved, or are there also phenomenological or epistemological differences?[17]

Marina is inviting us to consider that the appeal of scale shared by some Marxist currents or the fetish for locality by others distracts from a more profound question about revolutionary activity as it relates to space. Thus, we wager that looting as a *political* activity is always already an activity for survival, for "subsistence" in the emergent way discussed by Ross and cannot be scaled "up" as such; as Hartman implies, then it would just be accumulation. But looting and other non-accumulative actions can be the precondition for a different type of infrastructural and critical negation of the conjuncture, offering pathways to abolition along different vectors and metrics of organization, which in turn invites new questions of spatiality and temporality.

Marina asks us to confront the fact that our enemies are already scaled, up, down, and horizontally as well. They are planning for their future-present, betting and speculating on it, and we need not think about how to mimic that scale or appropriate the infrastructure along its capitalist scale, but rather about how to abolish the existing infrastructures by simultaneously appropriating and repurposing them for alternate uses. Marina writes:

> Management across scales can also imply management *of* scales, in the sense that management has the chance to develop into care: a reflexive undertaking rather than that mode of optimising activity or processes for predetermined ends called efficiency or performance. In this way management comes back to questions of scale from the standpoint of each specific situation. Scale is an artefact of the productive imagination and the specific engineering process in question, not a pre-existing frame of reference keeping a predetermined order that technology is designed to respond to, whether in an ameliorative or a punitive way.[18]

Thus, if scale is "an artefact of the productive imagination," to aspire to it prefigures adherence to capitalist totality, or liberal identitarianism which trades on a similar commitment to a different universality. Perhaps, class composition (emphasis on the composition) is a more meaningful way to begin to get beyond the question of scale. In other words, thinking of an activity like looting as a form of antipolitical action, as the participants of Volume 3 do, is one way to conceive of bridging critiques of political economy and so-called identity politics through the analysis of a form of composition. Totality is not something to be restored through modalities of collectivization, socialization, or nationalization, but rather "a web of violent domination to be abolished."[19]

Throughout the conversations that comprise the three volumes of *Diversity of Aesthetics*, we have endeavored to make space for thinking and action that goes against that web of violence, whether in the museum or at the encampment, and that creatively thinks against the limits of the "productive imagination" so intricately mapped by Marina. Our commitment to such a project was encouraged and inspired by her work, and we are infinitely grateful to her for asking these questions and pushing the conversation further. Thank you, dear comrade.

ENDNOTES

INTRODUCTION

1 The space has a storied legacy: it housed George Maciunas' last Fluxhouse (1975), then Olga Adorno and Jean Dupuy's Grommet Gallery (1982–1984), followed by Emily Harvey Gallery (1983–2004), the home of the Fluxus group.

2 See Marina Vishmidt, "Beneath the Atelier, the Desert: Critique, Institutional and Infrastructural," in *Marion von Osten: Once We Were Artists*, ed. Maria Hlavajova and Tom Holert (Amsterdam: BAK, 2017); Marina Vishmidt, "Only as Self-Regulating Negativity: Infrastructure and Critique," *Journal of Science and Technology of the Arts* 13, no. 3 (2021): 13–24; and Marina Vishmidt and Andreas Petrossiants, "Spaces of Speculation: Movement Politics in the Infrastructure," *Historical Materialism*, November 14, 2020, https://www.historicalmaterialism.org, an interview in which they discuss Marina's book *Speculation as a Mode of Production: Forms of Value Subjectivity in Art and Capital* (London: Brill, 2018; Chicago: Haymarket, 2020).

3 By "speculative," we refer to Vishmidt's notion of critical, negative speculation. She writes, "We have seen that speculative thought, like capital, is pervaded by a labour that it disavows and expels. Does this constitute a genuine shift in the subjectivation of labour that will take ever-greater hold in the persistence of crisis conditions, or is it simply epiphenomenal to a particular mode of neoliberal ideology? Central here could be that the constitutive indeterminacy of the aesthetic driving the speculative mode of production can become an active negativity, essential both for a rupture with that mode of production and for insti-

tuting the speculative as an engine of social change." Marina Vishmidt, "The Hard Labour of Speculation: Shaping a Reflection on Methods," *MaHKUscript: Journal of Fine Art Research* 3, no. 1 (2019): 7.

4 Here we use "incomplete" as both literal description and as a reference to Cedric Robinson's exaltation of the power of incompleteness as an alternative to liberal and antistatist politics. See Cedric Robinson, *The Terms of Order: Political Science and the Myth of Leadership* (Chapel Hill: University of North Carolina Press, 2016). See also Stefano Harney and Fred Moten, *All Incomplete* (London: Minor Compositions, 2021).

5 Kerstin Stakemeier, "Marina's Cues," *e-flux notes*, May 31, 2024, https://www.e-flux.com.

6 Andreas Petrossiants, "Preliminary Notes toward a Destituent Art," *Social Text* 42, no. 2 (June 2024): 35–52.

7 On destituent power, see Jose Rosales, "The Reality of Destitution is the Destitution of Reality: Preliminary Materials for a Genealogy of Destituent Power," in *Unworking*, ed. Peer Illner (Berlin: August Verlag, 2021); Marcello Tarì, *There is No Unhappy Revolution: The Communism of Destitution* (Brooklyn: Common Notions, 2021).

8 See Vicky Osterweil, "Property and Theft w/ Vicky Osterweil," *Death Panel* (podcast), April 29, 2021, https://soundcloud.com/deathpanel.

9 Matthew Impelli, "54 Percent of Americans Think Burning Down Minneapolis Police Precinct Was Justified After George Floyd's Death," *Newsweek*, June 3, 2020, https://www.newsweek.com.

10 The last US president to be elected with a higher popular vote was Ronald Reagan who received 58.7 percent of the popular vote in 1984.

11 Jason Burke, "Food aid convoy for Northern Gaza looted after delay at Israeli checkpoint," *Guardian*, March 6, 2024, https://www.theguardian.com. Emphasis added.

12 Page 101. Saidiya Hartman, *Diversity of Aesthetics: Volume 3, Looting* (Brooklyn: Andreas Petrossiants and Jose Rosales,

2022). See also Susan Ferguson's comments: "The specific form of totality that capitalism organizes . . . cannot be arrived at by simply assembling additive lists of oppressions or by reducing the material specificity of these oppressions to underlying class relations. Rather, such relations of domination and subordination are 'reciprocally determined, or co-constituted' through a logic of accumulation that is not simply one terrain of social conflict among others but a unitary system of enforced social comparison that materially reproduces otherwise seemingly incommensurable forms of oppression in integral relation to each other." Susan Ferguson, "Intersectionality and Social-Reproduction Feminisms," *Historical Materialism* 24, no. 2 (2016): 38–60.

13 See Rona Sela's film *Looted and Hidden* (2017) which investigates the Palestinian archives taken by Israeli forces during the twentieth century, which are now locked in Israeli military vaults.

14 Mustapha Khayati, "Two Local Wars," *Situationist International* 11 (October 1967). Emphasis in original.

VOLUME 1
INSIDE AND OUTSIDE:
INFRASTRUCTURES OF CRITIQUE

1 Guy Debord, "Report on the Construction of Situations: And on the International Situationist Tendency's Conditions of Organization and Action" (1957), *The Anarchist Library*, trans. Ken Knabb, https://theanarchistlibrary.org.

2 Kristin Ross, *The Politics and Poetics of Everyday Life* (New York and London: Verso, 2023), 2.

3 Kristin Ross, *The Emergence of Social Space: Rimbaud and the Paris Commune* (New York and London: Verso, 2008), 24.

4 Henri Lefebvre, *The Urban Revolution*, trans. Robert Bononno (Minneapolis: University of Minnesota Press, 2003), 19.

5 Andreas Petrossiants, "Inside and Out: The Edges to Critique," *e-flux journal* 110 (June 2020), https://www.e-flux.com.

6 See Vishmidt, "Beneath the Atelier, the Desert"; Vishmidt, "Only as Self-Regulating Negativity"; Vishmidt and Petrossians, "Spaces of Speculation: Movement Politics in the Infrastructure."

7 Consider for example the way the director of the Whitney Museum of American Art, Adam Weinberg, responded in 2018 to a large protest movement calling for the removal of Warren Kanders from the Board of Trustees of the museum. Kanders is an arms dealer and war profiteer whose company supplied tear gas and other munitions to police forces at the border between the US and Mexico and in Palestine. The nine weeks of art and action called in response, which eventually led to Kanders' resignation, are discussed in detail below. Espousing modernist notions of autonomy, Weinberg remarked: "Even as we are idealistic and missionary in our belief in artists . . . the Whitney is first and foremost a museum. It cannot right all the ills of an unjust world, nor is that its role. Yet, I contend that the Whitney has a critical and urgent part to play in making sure that unheard and unwanted voices are recognized." Quoted in Jasmine Weber, "Whitney Museum Director Pens Letter After Vice Chair's Relationship to Weapons Manufacturer Is Publicized," *Hyperallergic*, December 3, 2018, https://hyperallergic. com.

8 Lucy Lippard, *The Pink Glass Swan: Selected Feminist Essays on Art* (New York: The New Press, 1995). First published in *Heresies* 1 (January 1977): 82–87.

9 MTL+, "From Institutional Critique to Institutional Liberation? A Decolonial Perspective on the Crises of Contemporary Art," *October* 165 (Summer 2018): 192–227.

10 Stewart Martin summarizes this in *Mute* as follows: "In 1974, Gustav Metzger called for 'years without art' in order to 'bring down the art system' and, thereby, its legitimation of the state. Appealing to the model of industrial strikes and their effectivity, he called on all artists to engage in a 'total withdrawal of labour' for a period of three years, 1977–1980, during which they should refuse to 'produce work, sell work, permit work to go on exhibition, and refuse collaboration with any part of

the publicity machinery of the art world.' Metzger calculated: 'Three years is the minimum period required to cripple the system, whilst a longer period of time would create difficulties for artists.' He added: 'Some artists may find it difficult to restrain themselves from producing art. These artists will be invited to enter camps, where the making of art works is forbidden, and where any work produced is destroyed at regular intervals.'" Stewart Martin, "Art Strikes: An Inventory," *Mute*, May 1, 2020, https://www.metamute.org.

11 Kim Phillips-Fein, *Fear City: New York's Fiscal Crisis and the Rise of Austerity Politics* (New York: Henry Holt, 2017).

12 *L'art pour l'art* is a sentiment carried over from nineteenth-century aesthetic theory that professes art to be independent from political, moral, didactic, or other non-art and material concerns. The term is inexorable from the histories of European and US modernism.

13 For a short introduction and critique of Saul Alinsky, and his widely popular 1971 book *Rules for Radicals*, see Aaron Petcoff, "The Problem with Saul Alinsky," *Jacobin*, May 10, 2017, https://jacobin.com.

14 "Decolonize this Place is an action-oriented movement and decolonial formation in New York City. Facilitated by MTL+, DTP consists of over thirty collaborators, consisting of grassroots groups and art collectives that seek to resist, unsettle, and reclaim the city. The organizing and action bring together many strands of analysis and traditions of resistance: Indigenous insurgence, black liberation, free Palestine, free Puerto Rico, the struggles of workers and debtors, de-gentrification, migrant justice, dismantling patriarchy, and more. In some cases, we have used cultural institutions as platforms and amplifiers for movement demands, but we do not understand the transformation of these institutions as an end in and of itself," see https://decolonizethisplace.org/faxxx-1.

15 The movement started with a letter of protest written by the workers of the Whitney and then Michael Rakowtiz withdrew his work from the show. Nine weeks of art and action were announced by a large coalition of groups including DTP and

others, after which point eight more artists and groups resigned from the exhibition.

16 Hans Haacke, a crucial progenitor of institutional critique in the early 1970s, first displayed *Shapolsky et al. Manhattan Real Estate Holdings, a Real-Time Social System, as of May 1, 1971* at the Whitney Museum in 1971. The work is a large documentation of slum lords and their violent practices of eviction and misman-agement all throughout New York. He researched the work at public libraries and connected the slumlords to Whitney board members and donors. While the work was highly controversial at the time, it is now in the Whitney's collection, a canonical example of postwar US art history.

17 "Reciprocal readymade" comes from Duchamp's *Green Box*, a collection of notes—anticipating score-based work to a degree—that he assembled on scraps of paper while making his canonical work *The Bride Stripped Bare by her Bachelors, Even* (1915–1923), also known as *The Large Glass*. The note reads: "Reciprocal Readymade: Use a Rembrandt as an ironing board." The prem-ise being that, if a readymade is to defunctionalize an object by making it art, then the reciprocal readymade would be to take an artwork and use it to do something functional.

18 Strike MoMA is a large, collective initiative that began in April 2021 to protest the Museum of Modern Art (MoMA) in New York. The movement began with the publishing of "Strike MoMA: Terms and Frameworks for Struggle."

19 Vishmidt and Petrossiants, "Spaces of Speculation: Move-ment Politics in the Infrastructure."

20 Boris Groys, "On Art Activism," *e-flux journal* 56 (June 2014), https://www.e-flux.com.

21 Hakim Bishara, "Behind the Scenes of MoMA PS1 Exhibition, Artists Confronted Leadership Over Chairman's Implication in Iraq War," *Hyperallergic*, March 18, 2021, https://hyperallergic.com.

22 On May 15, 2021, as Israel escalated its occupation and eth-nic cleansing of Palestinians, Israeli occupation forces also broke into and raided the Dar Yusuf Nasri Jacir for Art and Research,

founded by Emily and Annemarie Jacir. Earlier that week, the center's urban garden was burned to the ground and littered with munitions canisters, bullets, and other projectiles.

23 Shellyne Rodriguez, "How the Bronx Was Branded," *New Inquiry*, December 12, 2018, https://thenewinquiry.com.

24 Mario Tronti, *Workers and Capital*, trans. David Broder (New York and London: Verso, 2019).

25 Mario Tronti, interview with Francesco Matarrese Greenberg, *Greenberg and Troni: Being Really Outside?* [documenta (13): 100 Notes, 100 Thoughts] (Berlin: Hatje Cantz Verlag, 2012).

26 Tai Shani, "Why Art Workers Must Demand the Impossible," *ArtReview*, September 1, 2020, https://artreview.com.

27 Strike MoMA, "Strike ~~MoMA~~: Framework and Terms for Struggle," *Decolonial Hacker*, April 8, 2021, https://decolonial-hacker.org.

28 Quoted in Alexandra Lange, "This New House," *New York Magazine*, October 8, 2004, https://nymag.com.

VOLUME 2
FOREIGNERS EVERYWHERE

1 Verónica Gago, Marta Malo, and Liz Mason-Deese, "Introduction: The New Feminist Internationale," *South Atlantic Quarterly* 119, no. 3 (July 2020): 622.

2 Michelle Perrot, *Workers on Strike: France, 1871–1890*, trans. Chris Turner (New Haven: Yale University Press, 1987), 4.

3 While there were many factors that sparked this wave of rebellion, the most immediate was UC's proposal of a 32 percent increase to tuition. In addition to taking over campus buildings, the university occupation movement also tried various tactics—perhaps most notably the occupations at UC Santa Cruz, UC Berkeley, and at UCLA to protest a meeting to finalize the tuition hike by the heads of the state's university system. See *After the Fall: Communiqués from Occupied California* (February 2010), available at libcom.org.

4 For example, the introductory text to the collection of communiques from the university occupations, "We Are the Crisis: A Report on the California Occupied Movement," makes explicit use of the vocabulary of communization and even dedicates an entire section to the subject.

5 Maurice Blanchot, "For Friendship," in *Political Writings, 1953–1993*, trans. Zakir Paul (New York: Fordham University Press, 2010), 134.

6 See www.asabsanj.com/asab.

7 The Iranian Green Movement (2009–2010) was catalyzed by the fraudulent re-election of Mahmood Ahmadinejad, an ultra-right-wing hardliner. The movement grew beyond protests against the elections and was the first time that slogans against the highest authority of the government, the Supreme Leader, were chanted in the streets. The movement consisted of different classes and layers of Iranian society but was largely limited to big cities. More than a hundred protestors were killed.

8 For an overview of opposition politics in Iran and its diaspora see Collective98's article, "On the Anniversary of the 2019 November Uprising in Iran," *Plan C*, December 7, 2020, https://www.weareplanc.org.

9 See: "'Wildcat The Totality'—Fred Moten And Stefano Harney Revisit The Undercommons In A Time Of Pandemic And Rebellion (Part 1)," *Millennials Are Killing Capitalism* (podcast), July 4, 2020, https://millennialsarekillingcapitalism.libsyn.com.

10 Claire Fontaine, "Existential Metonymy and Imperceptible Abstractions," *Human Strike Has Already Begun & Other Writings* (London: Mute Magazine/PML Books: 2013), 55.

11 Carla Lonzi uses the term "*soggetto imprevisto*" translated by us as the "unplanned subject" in *Sputiamo su Hegel* [*Let's Spit on Hegel*], published by Rivolta Femminile in 1970. It is the type of subjectivity that appears when women affirm their sexual, cultural, and emotional autonomy. Breaking the mythology of the opposition between two sexes, that was maintained at the expense of women, means showing how frigidity, marginality,

and exclusion are not accidents but side effects of sticking to the role of serving men and maintaining dependency on them.

12 See Claire Fontaine, "Towards a Theory of Magic Material-ism," *Human Strike and the Art of Creating Freedom*, trans. Robert Hurley (Los Angeles: Semiotext(e), 2020), 297–305.

13 Fred Moten and Stefano Harney, *The Undercommons: Fugitive Planning & Black Study* (Wivenhoe/New York/Port Watson: Minor Compositions, 2013).

14 See Afshin Shahi, "Erotic Republic," *Foreign Policy*, May 29, 2013, https://foreignpolicy.com.

15 Colectivo Situaciones, *19 & 20: Notes for a New Social Protag-onism*, trans. Nate Holdren and Sebastian Touza (Wivenhoe/New York/Port Watson: Minor Compositions: 2011).

16 "The feminist strikes are unthinkable without the very patient labor of assemblies, meetings, and programmatic elab-orations. Additionally, the assembly mechanisms of feminist organization are transferred to unions, art collectives, and migrant organizations, and even challenge the structure of political parties in everyday life. Thus, the strike as a political process provides a common horizon or organization and practi-cal investigation about forms of life and exploitation in specific territories." Verónica Gago, Marta Malo, and Liz Mason-Deese, "Introduction: The New Feminist Internationale," *South Atlantic Quarterly* 119, no. 3 (July 2020), 622.

17 Kafka's narrator: "One is tempted to believe that the creature [Odradek] once had some sort of intelligible shape and is now only a broken-down remnant. Yet this does not seem to be the case; at least there is no sign of it; nowhere is there an unfinished or unbroken surface to suggest anything of the kind; the whole thing looks senseless enough, but in its own way perfectly fin-ished. In any case, closer scrutiny is impossible, since Odradek is extraordinarily nimble and can never be laid hold of." Franz Kafka, "The Cares of a Family Man," in Franz Kafka, *The Com-plete Stories* (New York: Knopf, 2012).

18 Claire Fontaine, "Claire Fontaine, Selected Works & Interview," interviewed by John Kelsey, *fARTiculate*, November 19, 2010, https://farticulate.wordpress.com.

19 The term "existential homelessness" is inspired by Gyorgy Lukàcs' concept from *Theory of the Novel* of "transcendental homelessness" as the reverse of bourgeois cosmopolitanism and, today we could say, of globalization.

20 After the suicide of Mohammed Rahsapar (an Iranian refugee) at a German refugee camp in 2012, migrants and asylum seekers staged hunger strikes and organized demonstrations against Germany's policy of confinement. Refusing the statist reduction of every possible form of life to the single form of the camp, migrants and asylum seekers from various parts of Germany violated their *Residenzpflicht* in order to travel to Berlin and participate in the occupation of Oranienplatz and the Gerhart Hauptmann Oberschule. The occupations lasted from 2012 until a compromise between state and local officials was reached in 2014, with the promise of a fair pathway toward asylum status. In the end, most applicants seeking legal refugee status were rejected.

21 The Milan Women's Bookstore, *Sexual Difference: A Theory of Social-Symbolic Practice*, trans. Patricia Cicogna and Teresa de Lauretis (Bloomington and Indianapolis: Indiana University Press, 1990). The book's original title is a work of *détournement*, appropriating from Simone Weil's *Notebooks*, Volume 2: "Don't think you have any rights. That is, don't obscure or deform justice, but don't think that one can legitimately expect that things happen in a way that conforms with justice; especially since we ourselves are far from being just. Vertical Superimposition. There is a bad way of believing we have rights, and a bad way of believing we do not have any."

22 *Antideutsche* [anti-German] is a general term applied to a wide and heterogeneous assortment of radical left currents in Germany and Austria. In the 1990s and early 2000s, there was a major split between those whose supported Palestinian liberation and others, more prominent in many respects, who remained apologists for Israel. For a helpful introductory over-

view of the history of the *Antideutsche* current, see: Editors, "Editors' Note," *Mediations* 27, nos. 1–2.

23 Claire Fontaine, "Raising the Uprising," *Human Strike and the Art of Creating Freedom*, 269–286, 281.

24 The 1973 historic compromise was between the Communist Party and the Christian Democrats, essentially signaling the final defeat of revolutionary communist aspirations through the party. The historic compromise was proposed by Berlinguer (secretary of the Communist Party) under the political pretext of insuring stability to Italian democracy, that was actually threatened by the strategy of tension, enacted by the Italian secret services in association with American agencies, that were placing bombs and enacting terrorist attacks in order to attribute responsibility to the subversive groups and criminalize social movements.

25 Pietro Calogero became famous for the "theorem" that connected the responsibility of some academics who were teaching courses related to subversion and its history with terrorist actions. The magistrate from Padova listed amongst the reasons for the numerous arrests that he commissioned the "formation of armed association" and "armed insurrection against the State" asserting that the publications of Autonomia Operaia and other printed matter provided visible signs of guilt and complicity in this matter. Sixty thousand people were investigated and twenty-five thousand arrested in this operation, but his main theory that saw Toni Negri as the head of all the political subversive activities taking place in Italy, from the Red Brigades to the spontaneous libertarian social movement, was rejected. The controversial trial of April 7, 1979 was the most dramatic moment of the "years of lead."

26 *Gemeinwesen* is a Marxist category with a rather storied history. First used by Marx in his *1844 Manuscripts* to talk about the particular kind of social relation that would obtain under the social form of true, human emancipation, Engels would later employ the term as a synonym for the Paris Commune and in discussion of the relationship between the state and communism in an 1875 letter to August Bebel. More recently, the term has

been rehabilitated by the French ultra-left in the work of Jacques Camatte, for whom it is not *Gattungswesen* [species-being] that defines the social substance of communism because it is a category that remained uncritical of its humanist underpinnings. *Gemeinwesen* critically resolves dogmatic Marxism's humanist attachments. For a good summary of Camatte's influence and its consequences on Italian communist thought, see Cooper Francis, "The Passion of Communism: Italian Invariance in the 1970s," *Endnotes* 5 (October 2019): 248–304.

VOLUME 3
LOOTING

1 See for example, Your Lazy Comrades, "The Interregnum: The George Floyd Uprising, the coronavirus pandemic, and the emerging social revolution," *Haters Cafe*, January 7, 2021, https://haters.noblogs.org.

2 Vicky Osterweil, *In Defense of Looting: A Riotous History of Uncivil Action* (New York: Bold Type Books, 2019).

3 Eugene Genovese, *Roll, Jordan, Roll: The World the Slaves Made* (New York: Vintage, 1974).

4 See Saidiya Hartman, *Wayward Lives, Beautiful Experiments: Intimate Histories of Riotous Black Girls, Troublesome Women, and Queer Radicals* (New York: W. W. Norton, 2019); Saidiya Hartman, "The Anarchy of Colored Girls Assembled in a Riotous Manner," *South Atlantic Quarterly* 117, no. 3 (2018): 465–490.

5 Fred Moten and Stefano Harney, *The Undercommons: Fugitive Planning & Black Study* (Wivenhoe/New York/Port Watson: Minor Compositions, 2013).

6 At the time of recording this conversation, the United Kingdom was preparing enormous funeral arrangements to mourn Queen Elizabeth II.

7 Relatedly, see Adam Gabbatt, "Queen asked for poverty grant to heat palaces," *Guardian*, September 24, 2010, https://www.theguardian.com.

8 Billy Anania, "David Frum, 'Axis of Evil' Speechwriter, Should Shut Up About Benin Bronzes," *Hyperallergic*, September 15, 2022, https://hyperallergic.com.

9 Anna J. Cooper, *A Voice from the South* (New York: The Aldine Printing House, 1892).

10 Stephanie E. Smallwood, *Saltwater Slavery: A Middle Passage from Africa to American Diaspora* (Cambridge, MA: Harvard University Press, 2008).

11 Vanessa Veselka, "The Treasure America Scavenges from the Poor," *New York Times*, September 9, 2022, https://www.nytimes.com.

12 Sylvia Wynter, *Beyond the Categories of the Master Conception: The Counterdoctrine of the Jamesian Poiesis* (Durham: Duke University Press, 1992).

13 See Sylvia Wynter, "In Quest of Matthew Bondsman: Some Cultural Notes on the Jamesian Journey," *Urgent Tasks* 12 (Summer 1981), http://www.sojournertruth.net.

14 See Toni Cade Bambara and Louis Messiah's film *The Bombing of Osage Avenue* (1986).

15 Audre Lorde, "A Question of *Essence*," Our *Dead Behind Us* (New York: W. W. Norton, 1986), 62.

16 On "nation language," see Edward Kamau Brathwaite, *History of the Voice: The Development of Nation Language in Anglophone Caribbean Poetry* (London: New Beacon Books, 1984).

17 The novel is based on the Wilmington Riots, an insurrection and massacre that took place in Wilmington, North Carolina on November 10, 1898. Hundreds, if not thousands, of black residents of the city were murdered. Those who were not killed were driven out, their land and other property stolen and claimed by white people. The government was replaced.

18 Butch Lee, *Jailbreak Out of History: The Re-Biography of Harriet Tubman & "The Evil of Female Loaferism"* (Montreal: Kersplebedeb, 2015).

CONCLUSION:
THINKING WITH MARINA

1 Mauvaise Troupe Collective, *The Zad and NoTav: Territorial Struggles and the Making of a New Political Intelligence*, ed. and trans. Kristin Ross (New York and London: Verso, 2018), xxii.

2 Kristin Ross, *The Commune Form: The Transformation of Everyday Life* (New York and London: Verso, 2024), 6.

3 Ross, *The Commune Form*, 39.

4 Ross, *The Commune Form*, 40.

5 As Danny Hayward shared with us, "Marina was very suspicious of one conventionalised usage of survival which she saw as falling under the broader rubric of reproductive realism." This is to say that Marina encourages us to be mindful of thinking about survival as a political end, rather than as a means for reorganizing shared values, and to resist the individualizing urge, which as Danny puts it, "disguises itself under the heading of a putative 'materialism.'" Danny Hayward, personal correspondence with the authors, July 11, 2024.

6 Mira Mattar and Julia Calver, "Activated Negativity: An Interview with Marina Vishmidt," *Makhzin*, no. 2 (April 2016), https://www.makhzin.org.

7 Vishmidt, "Activated Negativity."

8 Marina Vishmidt, "Cameron Rowland," *Artforum* 58, no. 8 (April 2020), https://www.artforum.com.

9 Ross, *The Commune Form*, 64.

10 Ross, *The Commune Form*, 64.

11 Marina Vishmidt, "Accumulating Futures," in Eric C.H. de Bruyn and Sven Lütticken (eds.), *Futurity Report* 1 (Berlin: Sternberg Press/MIT, 2020).

12 M. E. O'Brien and Eman Abdelhadi, *Everything for Everyone: An Oral History of the New York Commune, 2052–2072* (Brooklyn: Common Notions, 2022).

13 Nanni Balestrini, *Blackout* (Oakland: Commune Editions, 2017).

14 Ross, *Commune Form*, 89.

15 Ross, *Commune Form*, 88.

16 Fred Moten, Stefano Harney, Sandra Ruiz, and Hypatia Vourloumis, "Resonances: A Conversation on Formless Formation," *e-flux Journal* 121 (October 2021), https://www.e-flux.com.

17 In reading this section, Danny Hayward remarked that the line by Marina quoted earlier—"Today, the valorization process can shift from forced labor to self-branding and back, and capital becomes ever more 'humanized' in proportion to its capacity to destroy all life"—is helpful in thinking through the problems of scale. He writes: "To talk about scale under capital is to talk in a 'humanized,' or, rather, anaesthetized way about despoliation and ruination; then the question becomes about how to expand struggle without reproducing the fixed set of relations or proportions that obtain under present circumstances." Danny Hayward, personal correspondence with the authors, July 11, 2024.

18 Marina Vishmidt, "Pure Maintenance," *South as a State of Mind* 10 (Summer/Fall 2018), 88. Thank you to Danny Hayward for lovingly bringing this text to our eyes.

19 Kevin Floyd et al., "Introduction: Totality Inside Out," in *Totality Inside Out: Rethinking Crisis and Conflict under Capital*, ed. Kevin Floyd, Jen Hedler Phillis, and Sarika Chandra (New York: Fordham University Press, 2022), 5–6.

ACKNOWLEDGMENTS

Every undertaking is a collective endeavor, but this is especially the case with this project, for which investigation into the forms of militant social practice was the reason for gathering and the ethos of the production of the books, from the initial ideas through to distribution. Thank you to the participants of each conversation for sharing their time and for being a part of this project: Claire Fontaine, Iman Ganji, Saidiya Hartman, Michael Rakowitz, Christina Sharpe, Shellyne Rodriguez, Stevphen Shukaitis, and Rinaldo Walcott. Marina Vishmidt was a guiding light and crucial interlocuter at every stage of this project, and we dedicate this project to her. We are still overjoyed that Vicky Osterweil agreed to moderate and conceive of the third volume, which remains a crucial document for thinking through the 2020 rebellions and beyond. As Vicky noted in her acknowledgments to Volume 3, Rissa Hochberger's gorgeous design of the individual volumes was key to the distribution of the project. We are lucky to have worked with Josh MacPhee whose work we have admired for very long and we thank him for gracing this iteration with such a beautiful cover and layout. We thank Nitasha Dhillon for allowing us to borrow her phrasing to title this series. Danny Hayward provided brilliant comments and considerations on the concluding section of this book—we thank him and share our love and solidarity. Elvia Wilk gifted us with rigorous copyediting of all three volumes and incisive comments on the project from day one. Mariana Silva provided crucial help with finalizing the design of Volume 2 and support throughout the project. Christian Xatrec deserves special mention for initially inviting us to embark on this project and for supporting it along with the Emily Harvey Foundation. Andrew Weiner also provided support, thank you! We are grateful to all the shops, comrades, occupied spaces, and anyone else who helped distribute copies of the volumes, in particular Common Notions Press for distributing Volume 3 in the US, and Noah Brehmer and Dabartis who have helped bring copies of *Diversity of Aesthetics* to many anarchist bookfairs! Thank you to Olia Sosnovskaya for organizing the launch event for volume 3 in Vienna. And of course, a huge note of gratitude to our friends at Common Notions for agreeing to work on this combined volume. Thank you, Malav Kanuga, Erika Biddle, and Syd Rainer for believing in the project, offering such generative edits, and for stewarding this publication. We could not be prouder to feature among the remarkable, revolutionary, creative publications they have brought into this world.

ABOUT THE EDITORS AND CONTRIBUTORS

THE EDITORS

Andreas Petrossiants is a writer and editor living in New York. His work has appeared in *Historical Materialism, Social Text, New Inquiry, New York Review of Architecture, AJ+ Subtext, Frieze*, Bookforum.com, *Roar Magazine*, the Verso blog, *The Brooklyn Rail, Hyperallergic*, and *e-flux journal*, where he is the associate editor. He is a PhD candidate in Performance Studies at New York University where he is researching anti-eviction, squatting, and tenants' movements as they relate to the production of social space.

Jose Rosales is a journalist and independent researcher working on the history of revolutionary theory and its relationship to the collective practices that have recently emerged within contemporary social movements. Their writing can be found in *Double Binds of Neoliberalism: Theory and Culture After 1968, Unworking* (August-Verlag), *Angry Workers of the World, Blind Field, La Deleuziana, Deleuze and Guattari Studies Journal, Revista Punkto, SŪNZĬ BĪNGFǍ*, and *e-flux Notes* among others.

ABOUT THE CONTRIBUTORS

Claire Fontaine is a feminist, conceptual artist, founded in Paris in 2004, currently living and working in Palermo, Sicily.

Iman Ganji is a writer and scholar in exile and holds a PhD in performance and theatre studies from Freie Universität Berlin. From 2004 to 2012, he lived in Tehran, where he worked as a translator, writer, and activist, co-translating books by Spinoza, Marx, Benjamin, and others.

Saidiya Hartman is the author of *Scenes of Subjection: Terror, Slavery, and Self-Making in Nineteenth-Century America* (1997; Norton, 2022); *Lose Your Mother: A Journey Along the Atlantic Slave Route* (Farrar, Straus & Giroux, 2007) and *Wayward Lives, Beautiful Experiments* (Norton, 2019), which received the National Book Critics Circle Award for Criticism, and the PEN/John Kenneth Galbraith Award for Nonfiction, the Mary Nickliss Prize from the Organization of American Historians, the Judy Grahn Prize for Lesbian Nonfiction, and the John Hope Franklin Prize from the American Studies Association. She received a MacArthur Fellowship in 2019 and was elected a member of the American Academy of Arts and Sciences in 2022. She is a member of the Royal Society of Literature and a University Professor.

Vicky Osterweil is a writer, worker, and agitator based in Philadelphia. She is a member of CAW writers collective, maintains a blog at All Cats Are Beautiful on Ghost.io, and is the author of two books, *In Defense of Looting* (Bold Type, 2020) and *The Extended Universe* (Haymarket, 2025).

Christina Sharpe is a writer, professor, and Tier 1 Canada Research Chair in Black Studies in the Humanities at York University in Toronto. Sharpe is the author of *Monstrous Intimacies: Making Post-Slavery Subjects* (2010), *In the Wake: On Blackness and Being* (2016), and *Ordinary Notes* (2023)—winner of the Hilary Weston Writer's Trust Prize in Nonfiction and the Hodler Prize, and finalist for the National Book Award in Nonfiction, the National Book Critics Circle Award in Nonfiction, the LA Times Current Interest Book Award, and the James Tait Black Prize in Biography. In April 2024, she was awarded a Windham-Campbell Prize in Nonfiction and was named a Guggenheim Fellow. In May, she received the

Canada Council for the Arts Molson Prize for the Sciences and Humanities. Sharpe is currently working on *What Could a Vessel Be?* (FSG/Knopf, Canada 2025) and *Black. Still. Life.* (Duke 2027).

Stevphen Shukaitis is Reader at the University of Essex and a member of the Autonomedia editorial collective. Since 2009 he has coordinated and edited Minor Compositions and is codirector of the commons research center COVER. He is the author of *Imaginal Machines* (2009), *The Composition of Movements to Come* (2016), *Combination Acts* (2019), and *The Wages of Dreamwork* (2024). His research focuses on the emergence of collective imagination in social movements and the changing compositions of cultural and artistic labor.

Michael Rakowitz is an Iraqi American artist working at the intersection of problem-solving and troublemaking. His work has appeared in venues worldwide including documenta (13), PS 1, MoMA, MassMOCA, Castello di Rivoli Museo d'Arte Contemporanea, Palais de Tokyo, the 16th Biennale of Sydney, the 10th and 14th Istanbul Biennials, Sharjah Biennial 8, Tirana Biennale, National Design Triennial at the Cooper-Hewitt, Transmediale 05, FRONT Triennial in Cleveland, and CURRENT:LA Public Art Triennial. He has had solo projects and exhibitions with Creative Time, Tate Modern in London, Wellin Museum of Art, MCA Chicago, Lombard Freid Gallery and Jane Lombard Gallery in New York, SITE Santa Fe, Galerie Barbara Wien in Berlin, Rhona Hoffman Gallery in Chicago, Malmö Konsthall, Tensta Konsthall, and Kunstraum Innsbruck, and Waterfronts—England's Creative Coast. He is the recipient of the 2020 Nasher Prize; the 2018 Herb Alpert Award in the Arts; a 2012 Tiffany Foundation Award; a 2008 Creative Capital Grant; a Sharjah Biennial Jury Award; a 2006 New York Foundation for the Arts Fellowship Grant in Architecture and Environmental Structures; the 2003 Dena Foundation Award, and the 2002 Design 21 Grand Prix from UNESCO. He was awarded the 2018–2020 Fourth Plinth commission in London's Trafalgar

Square. From 2019–2020, a survey of Rakowitz's work traveled from Whitechapel Gallery in London, to Castello di Rivoli Museo d'Arte Contemporanea in Torino, to the Jameel Arts Centre in Dubai. Rakowitz is represented by Rhona Hoffman Gallery, Chicago; Jane Lombard Gallery, New York; and Barbara Wien Galerie, Berlin; Pi Artworks, Istanbul; and Green Art Gallery, Dubai. He lives and works in Chicago.

Shellyne Rodriguez is an artist, educator, writer, and community organizer based in the Bronx. Her practice utilizes text, drawing, painting, collage and sculpture to depict spaces and subjects engaged in strategies of survival against erasure and subjugation.

Rinaldo Walcott is professor and chair of Africana and American Studies at the University of Buffalo. He holds the Carl V. Granger Chair in Africana and American Studies. He is a writer and critic. His research is in the area of Black Diaspora Cultural Studies, gender and sexuality with interests in nations, nationalisms, multiculturalism, policy, and education broadly defined. As an interdisciplinary Black Studies scholar, Walcott has published in a wide range of venues on everything from literature to film, to theater to music to policy. His articles have appeared in scholarly journals and books, as well as popular venues like newspapers and magazines and online sources. He often comments on black cultural life for radio and TV. Walcott has edited or coedited multiple works including *Rude: Contemporary Black Canadian Cultural Criticism* (Insomniac, 2000). Walcott is the author of *Black Like Who: Writing Black Canada* (Insomniac Press, 1997 with a second revised edition in 2003). He is also the author of *Queer Returns: Essays on Multiculturalism, Diaspora and Black Studies* (Insomniac Press, 2016) and coauthor of *Black Life: Post-BLM and the Struggle for Freedom* (Arbeiter Ring, 2019). In 2021, Walcott published *The Long Emancipation: Moving Towards Freedom* (Duke University Press) and *On Property: Policing, Prisons, and the Call for Abolition* (Biblioasis).

ABOUT COMMON NOTIONS

Common Notions is a publishing house and programming platform that fosters new formulations of living autonomy. We aim to circulate timely reflections, clear critiques, and inspiring strategies that amplify movements for social justice.

Our publications trace a constellation of critical and visionary meditations on the organization of freedom. By any media necessary, we seek to nourish the imagination and generalize common notions about the creation of other worlds beyond state and capital. Inspired by various traditions of autonomism and liberation—in the US and internationally, historical and emerging from contemporary movements—our publications provide resources for a collective reading of struggles past, present, and to come.

Common Notions regularly collaborates with political collectives, militant authors, radical presses, and maverick designers around the world. Our political and aesthetic pursuits are dreamed and realized with Antumbra Designs.

www.commonnotions.org
info@commonnotions.org

BECOME A COMMON NOTIONS MONTHLY SUSTAINER

These are decisive times ripe with challenges and possibility, heartache, and beautiful inspiration. More than ever, we need timely reflections, clear critiques, and inspiring strategies that can help movements for social justice grow and transform society.

Help us amplify those words, deeds, and dreams that our liberation movements, and our worlds, so urgently need.

Movements are sustained by people like you, whose fugitive words, deeds, and dreams bend against the world of domination and exploitation.

For collective imagination, dedicated practices of love and study, and organized acts of freedom.
By any media necessary.
With your love and support.

Monthly sustainers start at $15 and receive each new book in our publishing program.

commonnotions.org/sustain

MORE FROM COMMON NOTIONS

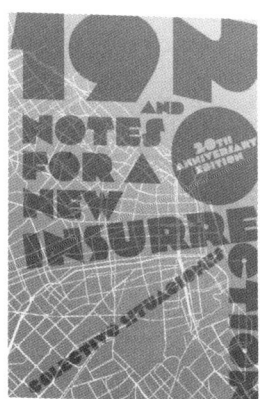

19 AND 20: NOTES FOR A NEW INSURRECTION
Colectivo Situaciones

ISBN: 9781942173489
Size: 6 x 9
Page count: 288
Subjects: Latin America /
Insurrections / Resistance

From a rebellion against neoliberalism's miserable failures, notes for a new insurrection and a new society.

19 and 20 tells the story of one of the most popular uprising against neoliberalism: on December 19th and 20th, 2001, amidst a financial crisis that tanked the economy, ordinary people in Argentina took to the streets shouting *"¡Qué se vayan todos!'* (They all must go!) In those exhilarating days, government after government fell as people invented a new economy and a new way of governing themselves.

It was a defining moment of the antiglobalization movement and Colectivo Situaciones was there, thinking and engaging in the struggle. Revisiting the forms of counterpower that emerged from the shadow of neoliberal rule, Colectivo Situaciones reminds us that our potential is collective and ungovernable.

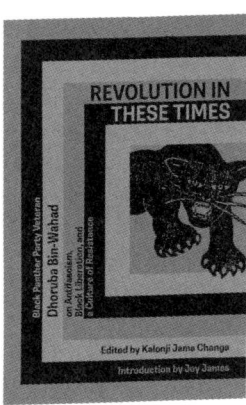

REVOLUTION IN THESE TIMES

Dhoruba Bin Wahad
Edited by Kalonji Jama Changa
Foreword by: Joy James
Afterword by: Bibi Olugbala Angola

ISBN: 9781945335136
Size: 5.5 x 8.5
Page count: 176
Subjects: Black Liberation / Radicalism / Antifascism

Lessons for the antifascist fight now and to come rooted in well-learned lessons from Black liberation.

Revolution in These Times delivers veteran Black Panther Party member, Black Liberation Army leader, and former political prisoner Dhoruba Bin Wahad direct in his own words to offer us an analysis of how today's resurgent right-wing agenda is an outgrowth of the ongoing and historical political struggle between the oppressed masses and settler-colonialism of America and Europe. Bin Wahad not only explores how white supremacist politics have recaptured the American imagination but also prescribes a radical grassroots response to counter this ideology and supplant the violent state repression that keeps it in power.

Bin Wahad pieces together fight-back strategies against the police and the state through a process of mobilizing in the streets, on the block, and in our communities, while gathering mass through antifascist coalition-building in a manner unrealized since the 1960s and 1970s. In this series of interviews, Bin Wahad grounds us in the now, seamlessly weaving together firsthand accounts of his own and other's revolutionary past in the history of struggle, alongside lessons for today.

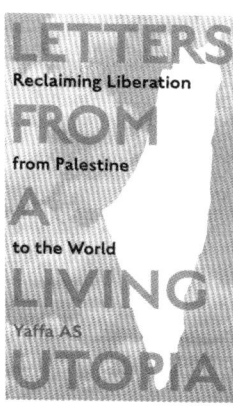

LETTERS FROM A LIVING UTOPIA: RECLAIMING LIBERATION FROM PALESTINE TO THE WORLD
Yaffa AS

ISBN: 9781945335303
Size: 5 x 7
Page count: 96
Subjects: Palestine / Utopias / Queer

A love letter to liberation, from Palestine to the ground beneath your feet.

When you think of freedom, where are you? And where are you headed? *Letters from a Living Utopia* invites readers to engage with utopia as both a destination and a lived reality starting with the ground beneath our feet. Dreaming of freedom from the displaced and occupied realities of Palestine, Mx Yaffa builds bridges between the historical struggle for liberation and self-determination and the everyday, intimate, and interconnected ways that we build freedom where we are, through care, healing, and bonds of solidarity. *Letters from a Living Utopia* is a remarkable journey to a world in formation, emergent in our resilience and our repair, our spiritual grounding and our non-attachment, our love and joy, and our sustainable and sustaining relations to the earth in its abundance.

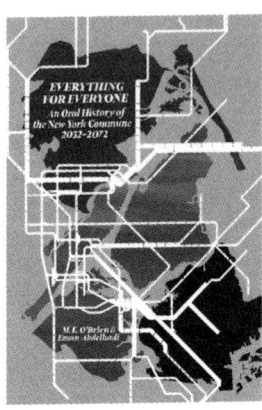

EVERYTHING FOR EVERYONE: AN ORAL HISTORY OF THE NEW YORK COMMUNE, 2052–2072

M. E. O'Brien and Eman Abdelhadi

ISBN: 9781942173588
Size: 5 x 8
Page count: 256
Subjects: Speculative Fiction / Revolution / Communism

By the middle of the twenty-first century, war, famine, economic collapse, and climate catastrophe had toppled the world's governments. In the 2050s, the insurrections reached the nerve center of global capitalism—New York City. This book, a collection of interviews with the people who made the revolution, was published to mark the twentieth anniversary of the New York Commune, a radically new social order forged in the ashes of capitalist collapse.

Here is the insurrection in the words of the people who made it, a cast as diverse as the city itself. Nurses, sex workers, antifascist militants, and survivors of all stripes recall the collapse of life as they knew it and the emergence of a collective alternative. Their stories, delivered in deeply human fashion, together outline how ordinary people's efforts to survive in the face of crisis contain the seeds of a new world.